Table of contents for the book

I0071528

This is a list of stuff that's in this book (aka the Table of Contents)

Foreword Thingy:

I guess this is stuff I'm supposed to say before the book begins. Actually, I'm too lazy to write this, so I asked some of my friends (all whom I know will be "a really big deal" in the near future) to write nice stuff about me.

"Neville is my hero. Most entrepreneurs closely guard the keys to their success, hoarding their hard-fought knowledge as if they were the spoils of war. This book is the latest and greatest in a series of steps that Neville has always taken to allow us all to peek into his brain; the brain of an extreme-entrepreneur that finds a way to be resourceful and question-the-status-quo in every life situation.

The brain of an entrepreneur that is just as comfortable trying to profit from zombies in an apocalypse as he is with an advanced e-commerce company."

-Tarun Nimmagadda
-COO of Mutual Mobile

"I wanted to share a story about Neville but I don't think a story will do him justice.

Neville is the guy your girlfriend prefers you don't hang out with.

He's a person if you just read his blog and his posts would assume he is totally bat-shit crazy (realize I say this with love and as a close friend of his.)

At the end of the day what you may not know about Neville is that he is one of the most reliable and genuine people I know.

He lives his life the way he wants, treats his friends well and is always willing to do something crazy.

This book will be the one you tell your friends, "Oh yea, I couldn't put this book down about some Indian guy doing wild stuff."

-Noah Kagan
-Chief Sumo of AppSumo, #30 at Facebook, #3 at Mint, founder of Gambit.

"Somewhere over the Atlantic Ocean at 37,000 feet seems like a fitting place to write a foreword for Neville's book. All the passengers around me are fast asleep in their lush "lie flat" business class seats. Even the flight's Relief Pilot seated to the immediate right manages to get some rest despite my laptop's glow. I'm almost always too excited to sleep on international flights. Partly, it's because as a private pilot I enjoy staring at the moving map fantasizing that I'm the one commanding the Boeing 777 over the frigid waters below. More so, is that long-haul flying offers the opportunity to work on the type of things that aren't normally a priority. Think about it: no distractions, people keep bringing you food & drinks, and internet is non-existent. Why waste the time on sleep?

This flight in particular is an extra fitting setting for reflecting on Neville. I first came across Nev's financial blog 7 years earlier while still in High School. Based on reading this blog I immediately identified with him as someone who took the path less travelled. A couple years later when we met in person by serendipity, my initial reactions about him were only strengthened. It is rare to meet an entrepreneur like Neville who is only at his best when in the entrepreneurial role. Neither Neville, nor myself could ever be content working for someone else. What makes our friendship even more unique is that Neville and I knew each other several years before I started Mutual Mobile. In many ways his blog and our personal conversations over the years contributed to the resolve that I have as entrepreneur.

If it were daylight I would be able to see Iceland out the left window. Instead I see blackness and am left thinking back to the reason behind my 5,000 mile journey from Austin to London. By all accounts Mutual Mobile doesn't need a London office. We already have the world's most renowned companies seeking us out on a daily basis irrespective of geography. There are still thousands of battles to fight and optimizations back stateside for MM that surely would be a better use of my time. In many ways my desire to create a London office is analogous to Nev's motivation behind his various experiments. My intuition says that having physical presence in Europe could lead to an order of magnitude increase in our European business.

A good business experiment seeks to test a possibly huge opportunity without requiring an equally huge initial investment. The administering of such business experiments is abnormal. All too often I see clients, business associates, and even friends wishing to irresponsibly invest everything they have in executing their new billion dollar idea. I admire their conviction, but not their methodology. Nev and I both subscribe to the concept that you can test pretty much any business idea without a little bit of money and more importantly a little bit of time. A good experiment will tell you with a high level of accuracy if the idea is worth adding increased quantities of both ingredients.

Given that our wheels touch down at Heathrow at 6AM local time and my first meeting (experiment) is at 8, maybe it actually makes to lie my seat flat and catch a few hours of shuteye. Emulating the types of business experiments that Nev conducts in his book will lead you down a path less travelled. And I can attest first hand that it is the less travelled path most likely to take you where you want to go in life."

-John Arrow
-CEO of Mutual Mobile

"In Neville's book, an experiment fails only when you don't try it.

This book is not to be used as surrogate for your own life experiences. Use it as the kick-the-ass inspiration you needed to start creating yours. After you finish this book, go out and conduct at least seven real-world experiments of your own. If one month passes, and you still have not started, kindly pass this book along to someone who is less afraid to act.

Do not worry about how clever you think your first seven experiments are. Doing what you think about is far more important than thinking about what you do. Action is above all else.

I have a lot more to say on the matter, but Neville also taught me the value of being concise."

=)

Regards,
Mickey Ristroph
CTO of Mutual Mobile

A quick intro

How a stupid blog I made (which I NEVER thought anyone would read) was the first financial blog on the Internet.

In college I did all these small "money hustles"…..most of them online, some offline.

These were extremely fun to do….and I really hated the idea of "forgetting" about all of them in the future. hrexcm

I figured a blog-style webpage would be great to document these things. It would also be a great way to document all the money I made from these random projects.

The idea behind this was:

> *"What gets measured, gets managed"*
> -Peter Drucker

I figured tracking my income would help **increase** it.

ANWHOOZLE….

I started publishing what I did online (mainly for myself), but lo-and-behold other people started reading.

Apparently no one had ever really started a "money blog" quite the way I had:
- I openly listed the income I made from different projects.
- I openly showed how everything worked, including full numbers and names.
- I did not hide behind a fake name.
- All my personal information was available for everyone to see.

I had inadvertently created a kind of "Financial Voyeurism" website.

People who read the blog sometimes couldn't believe I had the nerve to just post all this stuff up for everyone to see. But I was a dumb, young college student, so I honestly didn't give a f-heck.

WHATEVER.

Somehow this was interesting enough to where 3,500 unique people per day would checkout the blog.

This was despite my lazy attitude towards posting. Sometimes it was frequent; sometimes there was a month+ delay in posts.

But whenever I wrote, I always took a long time to make sure the blog posts were good.

It was a labor of love.

I never intended to make money through the blog….in fact….I actively MADE SURE I didn't make money from it for years!

(Boy….that was stupid)……

Anyhow, I started doing random **"experiments"** on the blog for fun. These were usually part money experiment, part social experiment.

This book takes seven of those money-experiments and lays them out here.

IN FACT **this book itself was an experiment!** I wanted to create "A book in two weeks"…..so I wrote, compiled and edited this book in two weeks.

This means you're almost guaranteed to see spelling mistakes, grammar mishaps and somewhat shoddy writing.

Screw it!

The point of this book is to take these fun experiments and share them so they MOTIVATE OTHERS.

Every successful person I know just "DOES" stuff. If they have an idea, they ACT on it. They do this over and over till they find something that works.

Every time they do a new project, they get better at it, they learn from their past mistakes and successes.

Every successful person I know tried out at least 2 to 10 crappy little businesses hustles before they hit it big. And I encourage all new entrepreneurs to just DO something….no matter how stupid and crappy.

You'll learn more by trying to make just $100 from a crappy little business than sitting around and trying to come up with the best business in the world.

So long as at least ONE of these "experiments" motivates you to get off your doughy bum and "just try stuff" I'll be a happy little monkey!

With that......YOU'RE OFF!

Chapter 1
The Bottled Water Experiment

How I proved you can take $5.00 and multiply it within 30 minutes ....and even got a bum on the side of the road to help me do it!

The little saga I call *"The Bottled Water Experiment"* was just another stupid idea that seemed like it would be fun to do....then publish on my blog.

....but it turned out to get far more attention than I expected! When I'd meet certain CEO's and people I admire and mentioned this experiment....they would hang on every word!

It turned into a social-secret-weapon for me!

So I'll first setup the premise around this little adventure for you:

Around this time, a lot of other "financial blogs" had sprung up like mine....and people would do these "Financial Experiments" which were usually completely lame, such as:

"I'm going to sell an old camera on eBay experiment and see how much I make!"

-or-

"I'm going to buy $75 worth of stock experiment and see what happens!"

HOLY CRAP!! STOP THE PRESSES!! I have to make sure I carefully follow how much some dork in momma's basement makes off his 3 year old camera on eBay!!

....the point is, most of these experiments were just plain boring, and didn't involve anyone **actually getting off their ass.**

It amazed me how wussy most people are that they can't even get out of the house and do some PHYSICAL work or MANUAL labor to scratch up some cash.

A lot of these same wusses have the completely false mentality that:
"You can't MAKE money, WITHOUT money"

They make this seem in their head that someone must already have millions of dollars to make lots of money, or get out of the rat race.

….and a lot of these same people criticized a list of **"Make Money With No Money"** business ideas I came up with.

Most of the suggestions on the list were something like:
- Sell bottled water on the side of the road
- Mow lawns
- Powerwash driveways and houses
- etc etc…

Soon after I got people saying things like,

"This sounds like a good idea. Just go buy some water and sell it. You'll be in business in 15 minutes! On the way to the park, just stop off to get a Business License, Seller's Permit, and Sidewalk Vending Permit…"

These nay-sayers only think of ways that ideas WON'T work. But not someone like you…..

….you're smarter than that, and constantly think of ways you CAN get ideas to work.

I actually did address (and very easily get around) the permitting issue in The Bottled Water Experiment.

In fact….I also ended up GETTING A HOMELESS GUY TO MAKE MONEY with me in the experiment!

....so without further adieu (whatever that means)....let's begin!

Purpose of this Experiment:

To prove one of my "Make Money With No Money" business ideas could work.
To prove you don't have to have massive amounts of capital to get started.

Hypothesis:

It IS possible to take less than $10 in startup capital and make money.

The Experiment:

Buy a 24-pack of bottled water and sell it on the side of the road. Possibly utilize the labor of pan-handlers holding up signs on the side of the road.

STEP 1: Getting the goods

I went to my local H.E.B. grocery store the previous night of the experiment and purchased a 24-pack of Dasani water for **$5.99.**

I put the water in the fridge overnight to let it chill.

Step 2: Doing some quick research

I wanted to make sure if I stood on the side of the road selling something instead of holding up a "bum" sign, I wouldn't get murdered by a bum who wanted my corner (I really thought this at the time).

So on my way to a party one night, I stopped to ask a bum what would happen if I sold water by the highway alongside other bums, and it didn't seem like a pretty picture.

He told me, "You're a rich college student, and the guy at the corner is trying to get a meal, the hungry guy won't be too happy with you."

To get around this, I wanted to **partner** with one of the regular bums who knows the in's and out's of panhandling. I made an agreement to meet at 3:00pm with this guy, **William Austin** to sell bottled water with me. I told him whether we sold all the water or not, I would give him $10 for his help. A win-win for him!

Here's a picture I snapped of me and William:

The picture didn't come out so well, but in person he was all smiles and very jovial.

Now I also didn't want to get **arrested or fined**.....so a few nights ago I stopped to ask two very courteous police officers what they would do **if they saw me selling water without a permit.** One replied, "I can't speak for every officer, but personally I wouldn't bother you unless you start causing problems."

SWEET!

While this wasn't a full guarantee....I could tell the **absolute worst case scenario** would be an officer saying, "HEY, you can't do that. Get outta here."

So I now had a partner and no real threat of legal action. The experiment was on for 3:00pm on Sunday Afternoon!

STEP 3: Keeping the water cold

During the time of the experiment it was approaching 100 degree days in Austin.....but this particular day wasn't all that bad.

Regardless, I had to make sure the water **stayed ice-cold** for people buying it. Just SEEING that cold-condensation on a water bottle can makes mouths salivate for a cool sip!

So an hour before the experiment I bought two bags of ice for **$1.29** each. I packed the ice and water into a little cooler I had:

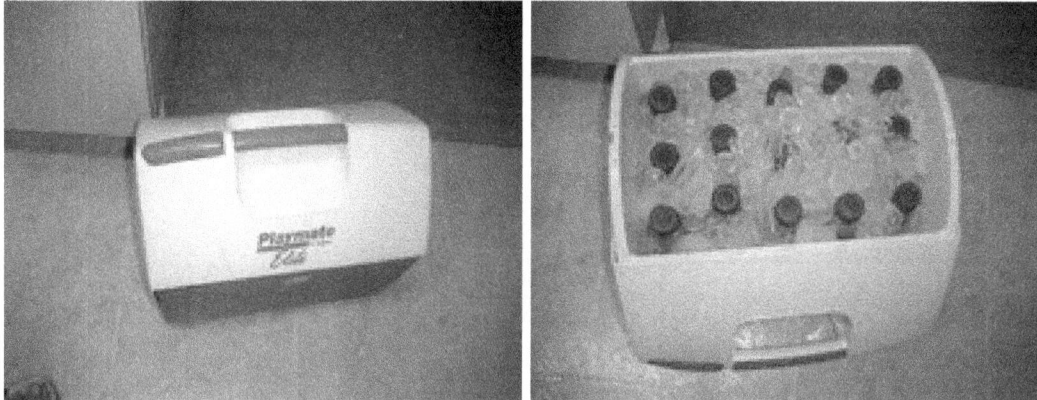

I could only fit **15 bottles** in my cooler, so I improvised and put the remaining 8 bottles directly into the ice bags. I then double wrapped them with clean garbage bags for easy carrying....it was like a ghetto ice chest:

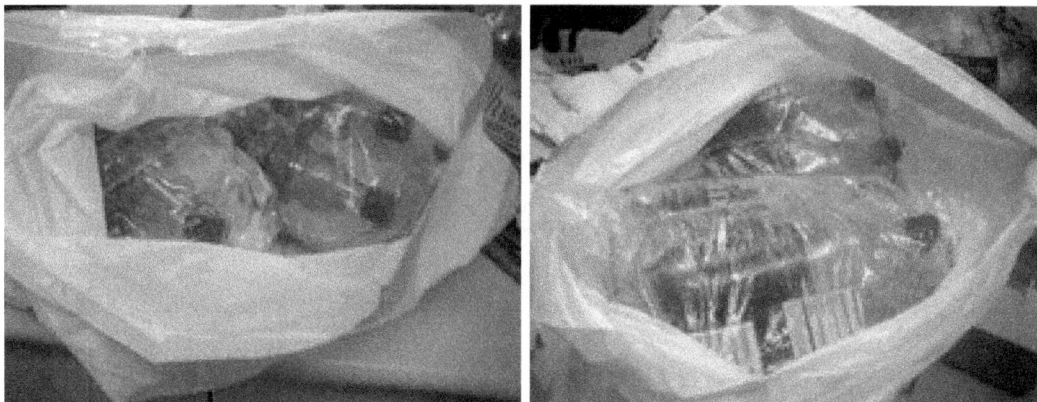

Step 4: Got some change ready

I got $20 in $1.00 bills in case change was needed to pay my bum partner, or if anyone needed to break some change:

Step 5: The "Water $1" shirt

I made this nifty **"Water $1"** t-shirt by taking on old shirt, turning it inside out (it had a logo on the front) and using a permanent marker to write on it:

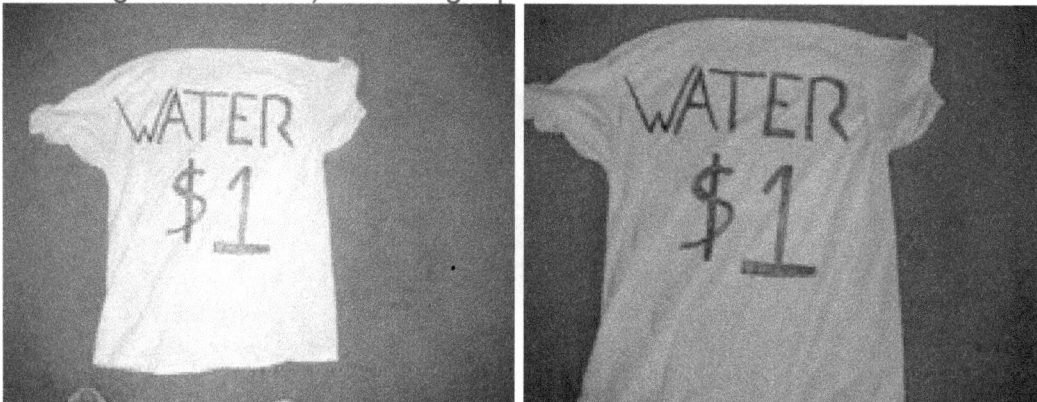

I had a feeling this little gimmick would work very well.

Step 6: Start your engines!

Went out to go SELL SOME WATER! I went to look for William Austin at 3:00pm by the local Blockbuster like we agreed. When he **didn't show up** I asked another bum to show me where he lived.

The bum leading the way (whom I'm absolutely certain was drunk at 3:00pm) led me under a nearby bridge where we found him. He was red-eyed and looked extremely tired. He also looked whacked-out on some sort of drugs.

He hardly remembered who I was and said he had to cancel on me (honestly he looked whacked out enough that I wouldn't have wanted to hang around him anyhow).

Here was the "house" under the bridge he made:

Step 7: Find another bum!

A bit disappointed my "partner" bailed on me, I went alone to the highly trafficked intersection of I-35 and Riverside Drive. I randomly met a bum named Barry:

I've seen Barry before. He's one of the bums that holds up **funny signs** like, "I gave up caviar for Lent!" and "I need new wheels for my limo!"

I liked the cut of his jib (sorry for the 1920's lingo), and decided he would make a good partner.....or at least an INTERESTING partner for this experiment!

I told Barry about my water experiment, and promised to give him $10 for an hour of his time, regardless of how many bottles he sold. He was more than happy to help. We shook on the deal and became instant business partners!

Step 8: Begin selling

I had a partner, I had the products, I had marketing materials (the Water $1.00 shirt), and I was standing on a street corner on a moderately hot day.

It was time to START SELLING!

Barry knew a little about water selling from people he'd seen do it before. He told me to hold three bottles at once and start walking down the idle lanes of traffic yelling *"Water Water Water!"*

Barry put the "Water $1" shirt on and started selling water like a champ! I stood on a different corner in my plain clothes and started selling. My first sale came within **6 seconds** of starting (and it was a $2.00 sale!)

Like Gary Halbert once said:

"If I was in a competition to sell the most hamburgers from a hamburger stand…..the only advantage I would want over my competition is:
A STARVING CROWD!"

Well it looked me and Barry had a DEHYDRATED CROWD because we started selling that bottled water left and right!

Get this:

In less than 30 minutes we sold all 24 bottles!!

Step 9: Calculating the results

I tabulated up the results, and here's what we got for this VERY FIRST experiment:

24-Pack Water	$5.99
Ice	$1.29
Ice	$1.29
Barry's Cut	$10.00
Total Expenses	**$18.57**
Total Income	**$24.00**
Total Profit	**$5.43**

BOTTLES SOLD:

Me: 14 Bottles (in yo FACE Barry!)

Barry: 10 Bottles

To make a better profit, one would need to:
Preferably perform the experiment by themselves, buy cheaper water, buy only one bag of ice instead of two, buy more than 24 bottles.

CONCLUSION:
You can indeed take an absurdly small amount of money and multiply it with just a little effort!

Now here's a little bonus……this is PART DEUX of the Bottled Water Experiment:

During the first Bottled Water Experiment I learned how to setup shop and shamelessly sell a product. The next item on my agenda was to **delegate that task to others while I do nothing.**

During the first experiment I met a homeless guy named Barry. He has a can-do attitude and also likes to make money. What he does NOT have is **capital and transportation**.

Well I do!

I recently tracked Barry down and gave him a proposal. If I set him up with several cases of ice cold bottled water and a couple of ice chests, he could sell the water all day (instead of simply begging for money) and we would **split the revenue** down the middle.

Obviously at first I'd get the sour end of this because I'll be **paying for everything**…..but I also don't do a fraction of the work he will have to do.

SO LET'S GET STARTED AND SEE WHAT HAPPENS!

The day before Part 2 started I went to Walmart and loaded up my car with **5 cases** of water and one **ice chest**:

120 bottles of water cost me $19.80 + tax. The cooler cost me $18.86 and tax.

Total Spent so Far: $40.22

Even if he sells all 120 bottles, I will barely make a $20 profit on the first run.

I then brought all the products home and began cooling them:

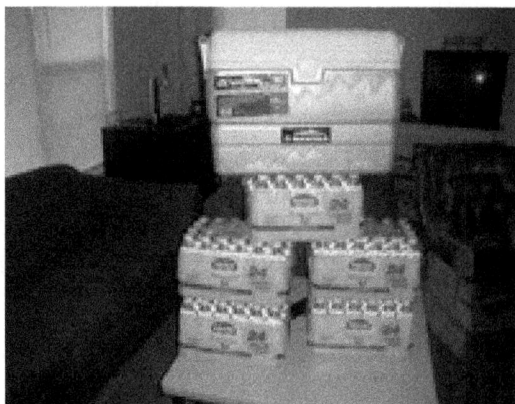

Each 24 pack case had 3 gallons of water and packaging:

1 Gallon = 8 lbs.

1 Case = 24 lbs.

5 Cases = 120 lbs of stuff to lug around.

I could only fit 3 of the cases for cooling overnight. The rest would be cooled in the ice chest later.

The next morning I met near the selling corner where Barry and I agreed to meet at exactly 10:00am. He showed up exactly on time (Seriously, the SECOND my watch hit 10:00am, he showed up riding a bicycle)!

Unfortunately for us, it was **gloomy** and **under 70 degrees** (I'm in Texas approaching summer…what the hell!?!)

I gave him another shirt I made that said "Water $1" on both sides. I forgot to take a picture but it looked exactly like the last one I made:

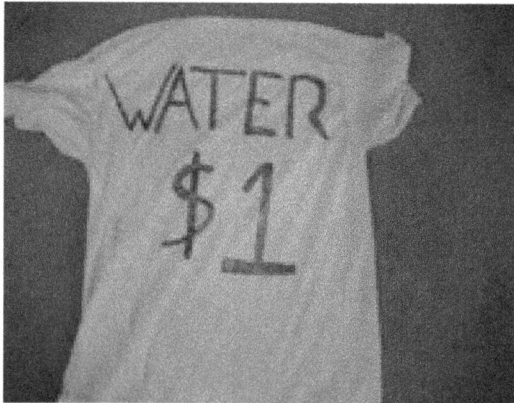

Barry then immediately started selling the already-chilled bottles of water while I made an ice-run (I didn't buy ice in case he didn't show up). I went to 7-11 and bought **40 lbs.** of ice, a sandwich for Barry and a spare box (the box was free). The total came to **$9.22**

Total cost of experiment so far: $49.44. The chances of making a profit are pretty much gone now.

We loaded up the ice chests with water and ice, Barry did most of the work.

I had got the spare box from 7-11 upon Barry's request. He had an idea where he would place the box saying *"Bottled Water $1"* further down from his starting point, informing drivers of the approaching vendor.

Before I saw what he wrote he said, "Damn, I spelled 'bottle' wrong and I misplaced the dollar sign." It was too late to change the spelling, and we both agreed the comedic value would probably increase sales!

Before I left for class, we took a pic together. A guy in a wheelchair took it. I accidentally had the camera on black&white mode. I only sold one bottle of water, and that was **on accident**. A taxi driver saw me carrying the **"Bottel"** **box**, smiled and pulled out a dollar. I sold a bottle before I even reached the median, without trying! Keep in mind the purpose of this is to delegate the grunt work.

Barry tried his best to look clean, I even brought him an old pair of shorts I no longer use.

FIVE HOURS LATER.....

I came back after he had been selling all day. He sold exactly 60 bottles, meaning we had 60 bottles left. The combination of cold + gloomy weather + Tuesday = not a great day to sell.

The fact that you can sell 60 bottles of water on a cold day made us look forward to the upcoming sunny, sweltering days!

We split the $60 in half.
Barry got $30.

I got $30.

So in the end I LOST MONEY. 49.44

Money Spent	$49.44
Money Earned	$30.00
Loss/Profit	-$19.44

Since this 2nd experiment, I repeated it about 7 times.

5 times with Barry, and twice with different bums.

They mostly made money, but it wasn't enough to keep up the effort (keep in mind I was juggling a full course load in college plus all my side-businesses).

However....I proved a point that even those lazy bums on the side of the road COULD hustle up money pretty quick.

A willingness to just DO IT is all it takes.

Chapter 3
Selling my school notes

How I took notes everyday in my college classes, then sold them for profit at the end of the year. Hundreds of extra dollars per class during finals time ain't bad! I wish I knew marketing better at the time....

There's nothing quite desperate as a college student during finals time....and I took full advantage of that!

You see....it's easy to sell something when:

YOU have something a group of people wants.
-and-
THE GROUP of people really needs what you have.

Well it just so happens that I'm usually a perfect-attendance student and take very detailed notes in all my classes. At the time, I'd argue I took THE BEST NOTES in all my classes because I had a tablet PC at the time.

This means I would use the software Microsoft OneNote (the most under-rated piece of Microsoft software ever made) to take notes.....and the notes were primarily typed, but they also had **digital writing and highlighting on them**.

My notes would look something like this:

[SAMPLE OF THE NOTES WITH HANDWRITING]
Show written notes with arrow pointing "teacher winked when she said we must know this for the final exam"

Friends of mine would often ask me for notes on days they were absent....and were always surprised how much better my notes were since I could mark-up the text with writing.

SO clearly by the end of a semester I'd have impeccable notes to study from (yet for some reason I still never got good grades).....

Now I went to the University of Texas which has in the neighborhood of 50,000 students, so some of my classes were rather large.

Small classes were about 25 people.
Medium classes were 80 to 100 people.
Mega-Large classes sometimes had 600+ people in them!

Some view these as "other students" ....I viewed them as "my target market" :-)

UT used a college-wide service called BlackBoard which is kind of like an internal version of Facebook for academic stuff.

So if the professor wanted to post your homework or grade results...they'd post it in BlackBoard, and each student could logon whenever they want and view the content.

Anyhow....BlackBoard ALSO lets students communicate with each other...so you can send an email blast to the entire class if you want.

::LIGHTBULB GOES OFF IN NEVILLE'S HEAD::

I decided to try selling my notes one year....JUUUUSSSST to see what would happen (plus extra pocked change is alwayyyss welcome to a college student). I had great notes in a small Asian Studies class I was in....**so that was my first target.**

Since all my notes were in digital format already, I sent out an email blast to the entire class saying something like,

> Hey everyone,
> I've attended class every single day and use my laptop to take perfect notes. I have detailed notes from every single class this semester, INCLUDING notes on when the professor "hints" at future test questions.
>
> You can even see 1-page example of the notes here:
> http://www.neville1.com/asia-notes.html
>
> All together the notes are about 30 pages long....and they make an EXCELLENT study guide for the final exam.
>
> If you would like the notes, I can send them to you in Microsoft Word format. Please send $5.00 to nevmed@gmail.com via PayPal and I will promptly send the .DOC file to your email address.
>
> -Neville Medhora

I actually don't remember the exact wording I used.....but it probably wasn't cleaned up and concise as the above.

ANYHOW....within two hours I got 6 people out of the 25 in the class who sent me payment!

Things were going swimmingly until someone else broadcasted this message to the entire class also:

"Dear students, I appreciate the entrepreneurial spirit shown here, but buying and selling notes is unethical!"
-Your professor

Unethical? Maybe.

Illegal? Not at all.

I knew I could win this battle, but she was a great professor and I decided to respect her wishes. I sent out another email retracting my offer to that class and apologized for any unethical behavior on my part.

In reality I wanted to keep selling the notes....but the professor ultimately had control over my FINAL GRADE, which at the time was much more importantly to me than some extra cash.

HOWEVER......undeterred by this little setback, **I realized the concept of selling my notes DID in fact work**....so I went on to another class!

I had a HUUUUGGEE marketing class. In any given class there were at least 400 students showing up in this huge auditorium.

The professor was Mrs. Cleveland and her nickname was "The Mayor" because of the obvious Cleveland city reference....and the fact that her classes combined had something like 600 to 800 students per semester!

Managing that many students must be like running a small city....hence "The Mayor".

The Mayor was actually a really cool lady....but also extraordinarily staunch on certain things (all hell would break loose if someone's cell phone rang during class).

Since the marketing class had us doing entrepreneurial-ish projects all the time, I figured selling my notes in this class would go over OK with The Mayor.

Almost every lecture of hers was closely based off the PowerPoint slides she showed on the screen....but she never gave out those slides.

So I would sit in class and literally copy word-for-word every slide in addition to whatever commentary she gave.

This meant by the end of the semester I had fantastic notes.

To add to the easiness of selling this class…it was frequently a class people "skipped" because it was so large they often didn't take attendance.

So towards the end of the semester I sent out an email blast like this to 600+ people through BlackBoard:

> Hey everyone,
>
> I don't know if you take notes in Mrs. Clevelands class, but I take lots of notes.
>
> I sit in the very front every single day, and have copied word-for-word every PowerPoint slide and commentary she gives on them on my laptop.
>
> I also make sure to write down when she "hints" something will be on the test.
>
> Every piece of important information in that class is in my notes. You can view a sample of the notes here:
> http://www.neville1.com/marketing-notes.html
>
> I am selling these notes for $5.00 a piece if you would like them. They are in Microsoft Word format.
>
> If you would like my full notes, please send $5.00 via PayPal to nevmed@gmail.com and I will promptly send the file to your email address.

At the end of the day I got 35 people who transferred money! DAMN!

An interesting thing about this marketing class, was that I first asked Mrs. Cleveland if I could sell my notes. I believe here official response to my request was, "SELL AWAY!"

It was a 180-degree different response from a lot of professors!

In fact I asked a History professor of mine if I could sell my notes…..and he said (and this isn't made up):

> "If you sell your notes, I will take legal action against you, and I will do everything in my power to get your dismissed from the university. That information is MY property, and YOU cannot sell it."

YEESH. Who knew making a couple o' bucks was so difficult!

I knew when this guy said I couldn't sell "his property" he didn't have much of a real legal case....but at the same time, I was at his mercy for my grades....so it was a battle I decided to lay down my sword.

I went on to sell other notes in further classes, all with similar successes and failures. Some professors didn't care (in fact some were GLAD I was profiting from other lazy-ass students!), and some were outraged at the thought.

SO IF YOU AND I WERE GOING TO SELL OUR NOTES, THIS IS EXACTLY THE FORMULA I WOULD FOLLOW:

1. Make sure to have great notes (this is good for academic reasons AND you can profit more if you have impeccable notes). Shitty product = unhappy customers. Avoid those.
2. Neatly wrap all the notes into a single file. Microsoft Word works well....or make a shareable document on Google Docs, and share access with only people who pay (this might be the easiest way....plus you can update the notes as you go).
3. Usually professors give out a "study guide" before a final. Complete that study guide....sometimes this is worth MUCH more than just the raw notes!
4. Send out an email something like this:

   What up class. I bet I have the best damn notes in the whole class. You'll be interested in this if you "missed" a few days:

   I've showed up to every class and taken detailed notes on my laptop....INCLUDING the little "hints" the professor gives whenever something might be on the exam.

   Ohh....I've also completed the final study guide and showed all my work and sources on it. This alone will help you immensely.

   Anyhow, I'm going to be selling my notes for [whatever class] for the next 24 hours ONLY. The prof might get on my case for this, at which point I will retract this offer.

   If you want my COMPLETE NOTES and COMPLETED STUDY GUIDE sent to your email in Microsoft Word format, do this:

   Send $25 to nevmed@gmail.com via PayPal. Here is a link: [Insert a PayPal payment link here]

   Happy studying!
   -Neville
5. Start collection orders! Cha-ching!

I made the mistake of charging only $5.00/piece in some classes. I now realize it almost doesn't matter what the price is. People will acquire these notes somehow if they really need them.

I'd say NEVER charge anything below $10.....and if it's very specific class, you can probably get away with a $50+ price point.

SOME FUN RANDOM THINGS WHEN SELLING NOTES:
Here are some actual emails I got in response to my email blasts:

"I don't want the notes, but you are very enterprising. Goodluck on the test!"

From: csonnier@mail.utexas.edu – Coby Jude Sonnier.
"i've got notes for free. the whole outline. hit me up and i'll email it to you cause i could care less about makin money like this guy. its in word so make sure you have it. -coby"

From: chillaxer0008@mail.utexas.edu – Jorge Eduardo Leal Jr.
"No deal, final offer is $2.50 for the complete study note. Considering your probably lack of sales with the study notes, here's your chance to make a sail."

"You just dont get it man,selfish bastard, stop trying sohard to make money,eventually everything will work out"

"go fuck yourself"

You're onto something good when you get the first "go fuck yourself" comment!

I only got a few hate mails (expected), but lots of orders.

Did you notice the poor spelling and grammar on the hate mail? Poor bastards...THEY could've used my notes the most!

The irony was one of the hate-mailers ended up purchasing the notes after he sent me hate mail! HA!
It shows:

"What people SAY and what people DO are very different."

Chapter 3
Selling Confiscated Stuff from the Airport

When they confiscate stuff from people at the airport, it all goes to State Surplus Stores….and this is how I profited from them.

Perusing Digg.com one day (a social bookmarking website) I found an article on Yahoo that explained what happened to all the **confiscated stuff** at airport security lines.

The article went on how the majority of the confiscated items were pocketknives or other sharp objects like box cutters and scissors.

Interesting! I never really thought about what happens to all that stuff….I presumed they just threw it away.

However that's not the case. What happens is:

Anytime items are lost or confiscated from a government-controlled building, they go to **State Surplus Stores.**

These are just big warehouses where they pile all the stuff, and the general public can go through and buy stuff….usually at pretty heavy discounts.

It's kind of like going to a Goodwill or thrift store, in the sense that 90% of the stuff is crap, and 10% of it might be decent. You might find 1% of stuff that is a diamond in the rough.

This sounded intriguing to me…..and I DO own a financial blog, so I figured this would make a fine financial experiment because in this case I could:

Buy stuff at a large discount.

-then-

Sell it at normal market price.

If I could get good enough discounts I'd make a profit!

So I looked up my local government Surplus Store...and it happened to be only 5 miles from where I lived.

It was called the Texas Surplus Store....and I'd never heard of it. In fact, it was in an odd part of town, and the building it was in didn't look like a place to go shopping.

It was a large ware-house like building, and I wasn't sure what I'd find there.

When I walked in the main entrance, there were large bins filled to the top with pocket knives, sunglasses, regular glasses, box cutters, tools and more random stuff:

Some of the other bins had large amounts of random jewelry.

Almost everything there was priced at $1 or $2.....which means if you get lucky, you can find some insane steals there!

While I was rummaging through the sunglasses….I noticed a really nice pair…..and found this $200 pair of Maui Jim sunglasses (and bought them for $1.00)!!

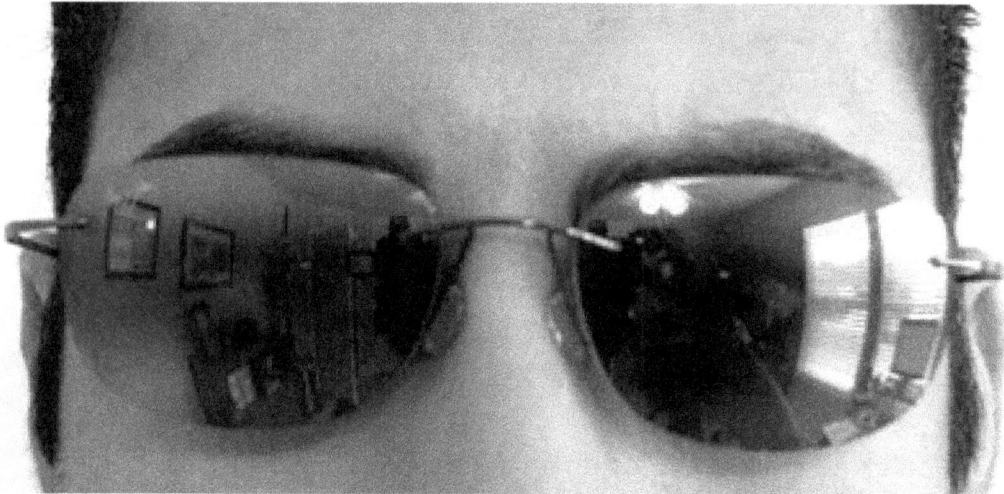

That was pretty neat….but then I realized another door leading out to a giant "warehouse" area.

I went there and it was a large warehouse FILLED with furniture, industrial machinery, cop car parts, file cabinets, pool tables, sewing machines and other random stuff. This warehouse was HUGE!

Everything there was either retired government equipment, foreclosed items, defaulted loan items or seized property….all at super discounted prices. These government surplus stores get all the stuff, and it's their job to get rid of it quickly. It reminded me of a big pawn shop.

Furniture, industrial equipment etc.

Emergency vehicle spare parts

This was rather interesting to me. I made a mental note if I ever needed extremely cheap furniture for a house or office....I would come straight to this Surplus Store!

So the reason real reason I went here was to see if **any money can be made from reselling these items** (most likely on eBay).

Something that caught my eye in the front room of the Surplus Storew were these big bags of assorted pocket knives for $10. I couldn't count how many each bag had inside, but it was a lot. So as a little money experiment I bought a **$10 bag of knives** plus **one Leatherman Micra** pocketknife for **$5** (just to get more keyword searches on eBay through the "Leatherman" brand name).

I counted all the knives, and it turns out I got **74 knives for $10**. The extra Leatherman knife made it 75 knives total:

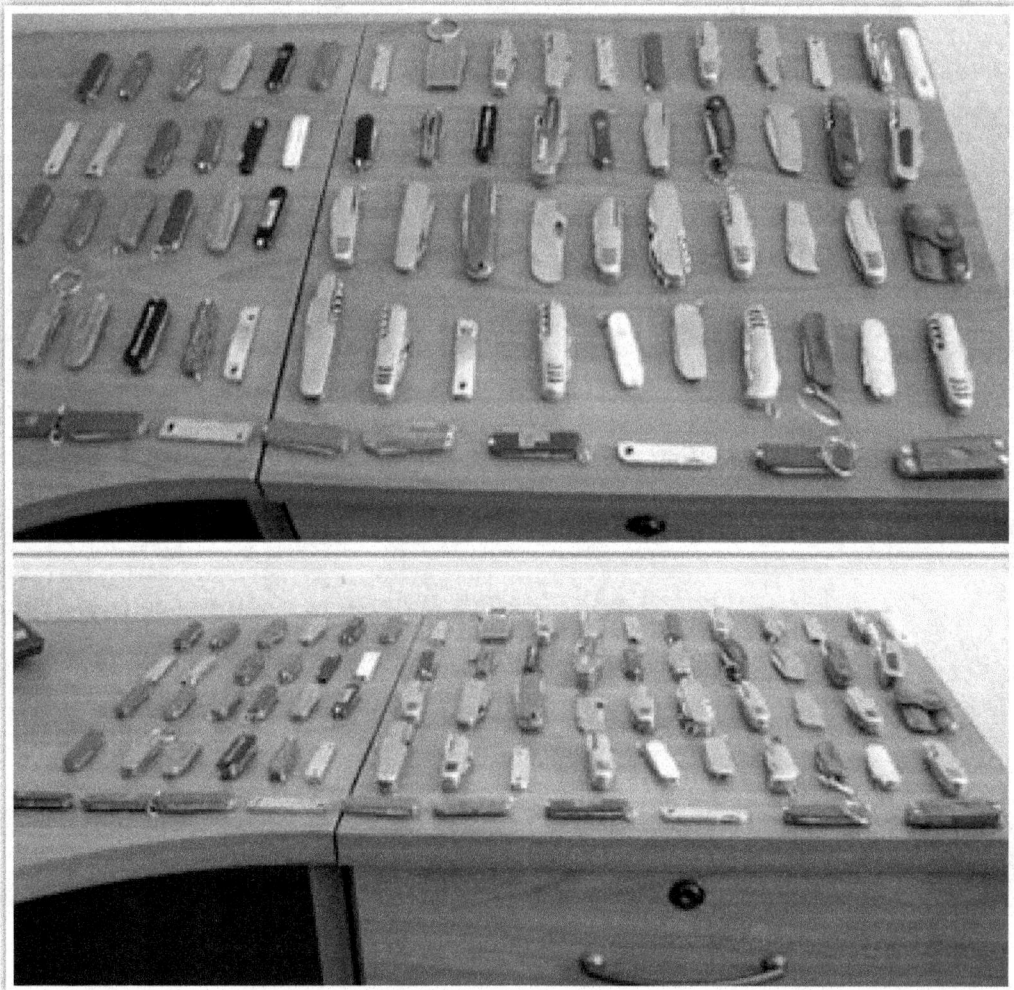

Thas'a'lotta knives for $10.00!

I took some pictures of the knives for the eBay auction, and I found out it's actually a pretty boring process trying to open up 75 pocket knives, so I just opened up some of the larger ones for a more dramatic picture effect. There were actually some very high quality knives in there, I was impressed:

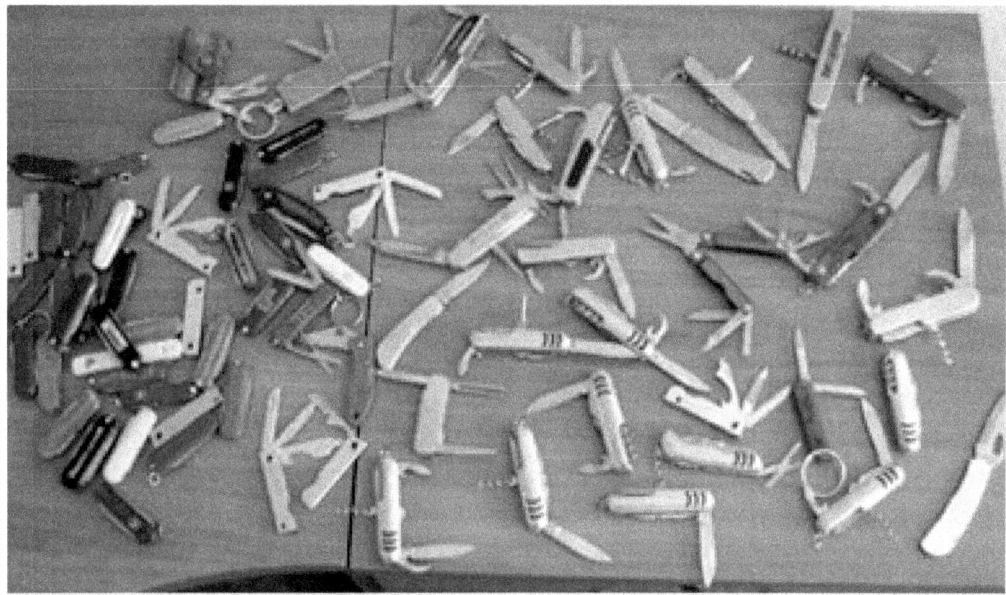

Then I went ahead and stuck the whole lot of 75 knives on eBay with a $10 minimum bid and flat $10.95 shipping charge.

I also went ahead and made a quick video of the knives, slapped it on YouTube and posted it in the auction.

After all the eBay listing fees and shipping costs…. Here was the breakdown:

It cost me:
$10 purchase price for knives
$12 shipping costs (although now I know a cheaper way)…..
$1 in eBay fees

Total costs: $23.00
Bought for: $37.50

Total profit: $14.50

Now I know that the U.S. Postal Service has flat-rate boxes with the motto: "If it fits, we can ship."

The small flat-rate box could've held all the knives, and the shipping would've been only $4.95 flat instead of the $12 I paid.

Also….this would be a great way for someone to sell products at a county fair or anywhere where you can get a cheap booth.

If you have a sign that says:

DO YOU HAVE A POCKET KNIFE?
PICK ONE OUT FOR ONLY $1.00

You can sell a lot of knives. Even a $2.00 price point would work fine….and if you recall I bought 74 knives for $10…which means about $0.13 a piece in cost!

From talking around to people I learned that there's people who make full-time livings brokering stuff from these Surplus Stores (although they generally sell the industrial equipment rather than the smaller stuff).

If you can find a cheap source, and a market willing to buy….you can make some $$$!

Chapter 4
The Scratch Lottery Experiment

How I spent $100 to buy $1 scratch lottery tickets…and actually made a small profit!

I used to live in nice student apartments a while ago, but it was in a soorrrt-of ghetto area of Austin.

It was at the grocery store across the street where I noticed that no matter HOW POOR some people were….they'd ALWAYS make sure they budget in **lottery tickets**.

This was amazing to me since I clearly know in my head that playing the lottery is for pure entertainment…not a rational way to make money.

Same goes for gambling….I've never been into it. It seems boring and pointless since you're playing in a casino which OBVIOUSLY has a clear advantage.

Anywhoozit….I also found myself occasionally buying those $1 scratch lottery tickets just for fun (they had a cool vending machine)! It even sucked in my rational-thinking self!

Now it's clear the lottery commission has an advantage, because they consistently make a profit. To prove it to yourself, look at the back of your next lottery ticket.

Often they'll disclose the odds of winning (or at least breaking even) are something like "1-in-4"

That would mean you'll win once, but lose 3 times. Clearly you are at a loss here.

This seemed easy to prove….and I actually thought it'd be pretty fun to try out a "Scratch Lottery Ticket Experiment"!

And it goes something like this:

Observation:

The popularity of scratch-off lottery tickets remains high despite their low odds of winning. The attraction of exponentially increasing an "investment" of $1 with no skill involved draws people to these games.

Hypotheses:

If a $1 scratch-off lottery game is played 100 times, the player is likely to lose money in the end. Most people playing the game will eventually lose money, only a few will gain.

Variations:

A player can potentially win a large sum of money on the first play with some "luck" on their side.

Experiment:

100 Texas Lottery scratch-off "Amazing 8's" games costing $1 each will be purchased. 20 games will be purchased from 5 separate establishments. Amazing 8's" have odds of **1 in 4.65 games at least break even.**

Let's BEGIN!

STEP 1:

I withdrew $100 in cash from an ATM and bought 20 Amazing 8's from each of these five establishments: Albertson's, Chevron, Diamond Shamrock and Exxon.

The whole process took me an hour as some places I visited did not have Amazing 8's.

On a side note, everywhere I went I asked if I bought the most lottery tickets that day. Almost every place said, "Ummm this is nothing....there's people that buy like ....50 tickets A DAY!" Yeesh!

STEP 2:

Counted and verified that I had exactly 100 Amazing 8's scratch-off lottery tickets. You can see them all neatly-arranged here (it took me a long time to lay them out...SO APPRECIATE IT)!:

STEP 3:

Got my trusty professional tools ready: **Two quarters!**

One is an American quarter and the other is a Canadian quarter. I found that Canadian quarters are much better for scratching mass amounts of lotto tickets!

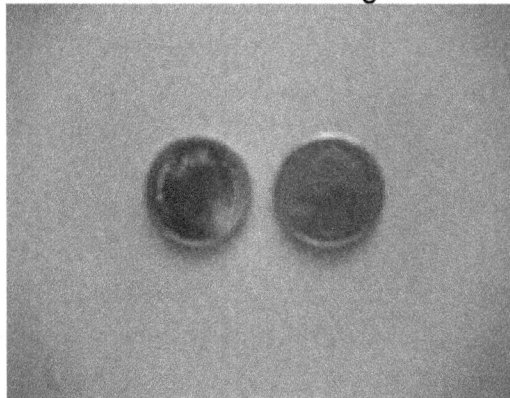

STEP 4:

Let's start scratching! I would scratch and scratch until I found a winner, which would then be placed inside the "Winner$" basket:

Scratching 100 lottery tickets is NOT as exciting as I thought. It felt more like a boring job. Next time I do gambling experiments, I'm goin' ta Vegas.

The "Winner$" basket.

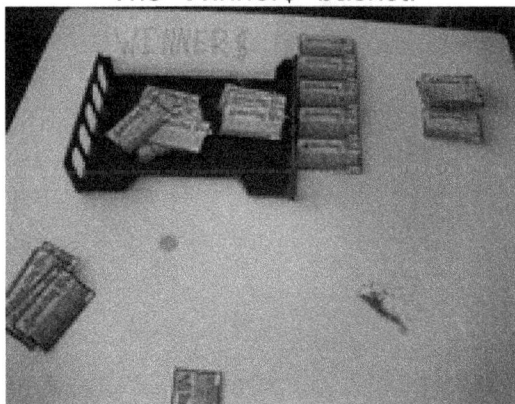

Winner$ basket starting to fill up with $1 and $2 wins.

The real gem of the lot was this ticket which **won $60!** The chances of getting this are **1 in 1,500** according to the lottery commission website.

STEP 5:

Tabulate each amount won:

Losers were placed on the table, and the proud winners were put higher up on the stool (Just for a more dramatic metaphorical effect):

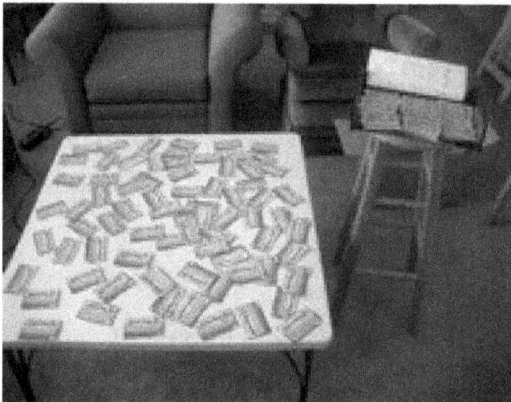

STEP 6:

Report the totals. **I came out ahead with $102!**

A 2% return!

Prize Amount	Number Won	Money From Each
$1	11	$11
$2	3	$6
$3	4	$12
$4	2	$8
$5	1	$5
$60	1	$60
Totals:	**22**	$102

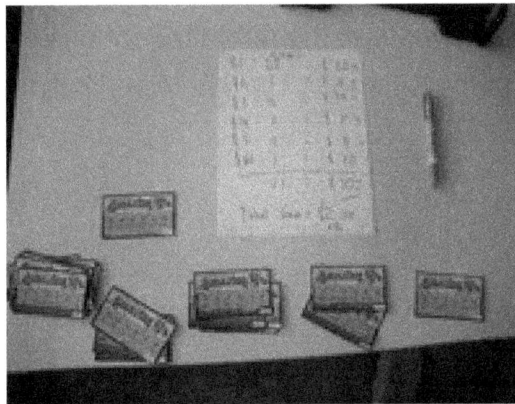

The proud winners in all their glory, especially our champion: Mr. $60!

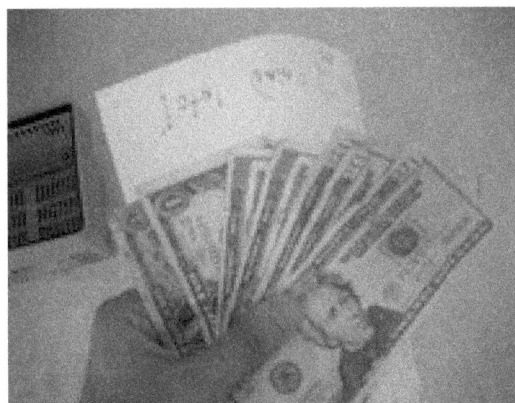

After the experiment was completed, I went to the grocery store to cash in my $102. I then proceeded to the Bank of America ATM and deposited the cash directly back into my investment account. So I performed this experiment and MADE $2 and learned a little too!

STEP 7:

Conclusion.

This "investment" of $100 was more of an **experiment** and should **not** be used as investment advice. Anyone who invests their money in the lottery for purposes other than mild thrills and entertainment is (according to the odds) **just dreaming**.

The odds prove that if you play long enough, you will lose 75% or more of your money. Of course you can also win a lot of money, but it's **highly doubtful**. I just happened to buy the right tickets at the right time for this particular experiment, but if I repeated the experiment again, I would most likely not make a profit or break even.

Hope you enjoyed the experiment, I sure did!

Chapter 5
Curb Painting

How I'd go out with a few dollars in supplies, and come back with a wad of cash.
By painting curb numbers on houses.

It almost seems like NO ONE of my generation has ever made money by hustling it up the old fashion way: With good ole manual labor.

I love the idea of a young person going door-to-door on a lazy Sunday afternoon and hustling up a couple hundred dollars in cash.

It seems so honest….so entrepreneurial….and will sure as hell be a better sales teacher than any business.

I wanted to show people who read my blog how to do this (and that even an idiot like me could easily pull this off), so I set about learning how to paint the address numbers on curbs.

So I set out on this little experiment:

I've seen people do this all day, charge up to **$40** per painting and do whole neighborhoods: **Re-painting the address numbers on curbs of houses.**

I always thought this was a cool and easy way to make some extra money. So in some spare time I bought some plastic stencils (About $8) and some black/white outdoor spray paint (About $10) and decided to see how hard it could be.

I took the materials outside and gave it a rough shot on some newspaper:

It was a little messy, and I had to end up cutting the stencils apart, but my first painting came out alright. Not perfect, but alright.

I then started using tape to seal any loose areas of the stencils together, and I successfully made a semi-neat spray of the numbers. This isn't hard stuff, but it takes a little trial and error testing.

I've seen lots of neighborhoods around Austin where I couldn't find a house because of the lack of address numbers…think of what would happen if a **police car or ambulance couldn't find your house number.**

I tried a live run on some old curbage at my apartment complex, and it turned out decent….very rough….but nothing a little practice won't clean up.

This would be an awesome way to make a good **$100+ a day** for a couple of high school kids or Boy Scouts. Actually, anyone could setup this little curb painting business for themselves and make a quick income! It involves an easy service you can sell door-to-door that people will gladly pay for.

It seems everyone nowadays is talking about "Making money doing nothing" …..which is great….but making money from good old manual labor is sometimes **very rewarding!**

My first tries of the curb painting were a little rough, and I wanted to actually DO this door-to-door, so I bought new materials and made my own custom curb border out of cardboard I had laying around the house. I was surprised how cheap everything was! Altogether my total at Home Depot came out to **less than $15!** Checkout the screenshot of the self-checkout line I went through:

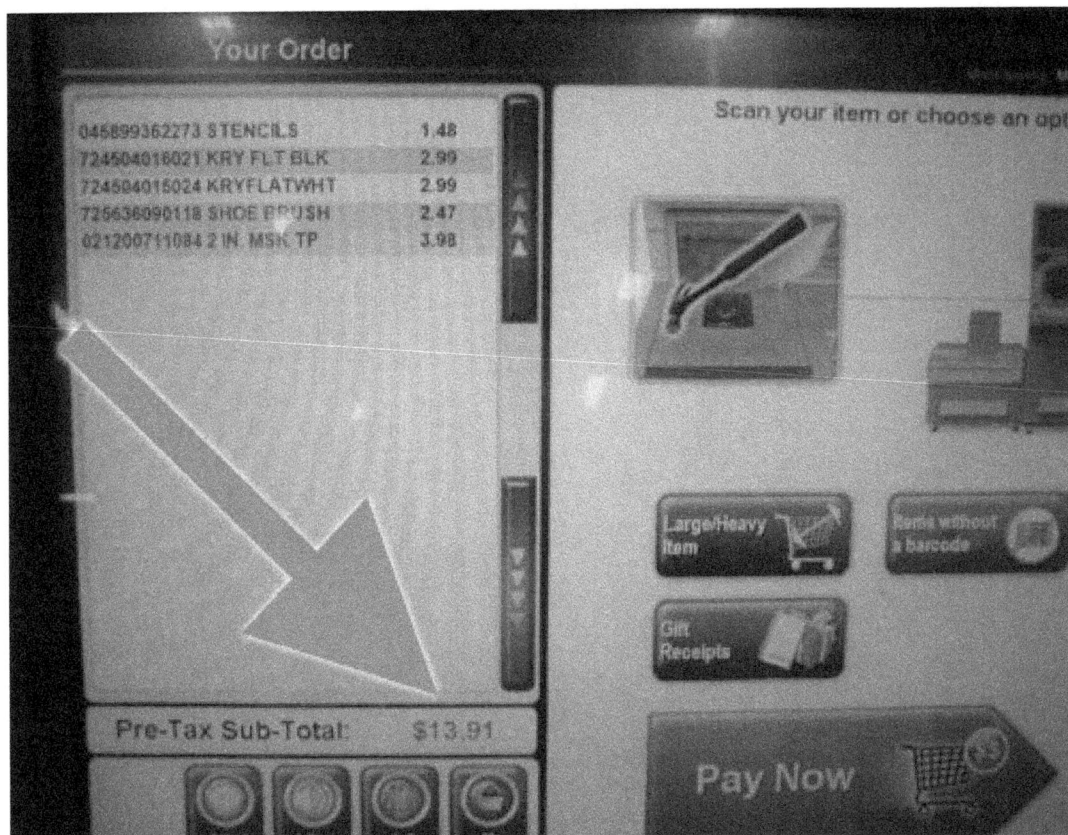

045899362273 STENCILS	1.48
724504016021 KRY FLT BLK	2.99
724504015024 KRYFLATWHT	2.99
726636090118 SHOE BRUSH	2.47
021200711084 2 IN MSK TP	3.98

Pre-Tax Sub-Total: $13.91

Scan your item or choose an opti

Large/Heavy Item

Items without a barcode

Gift Receipts

Pay Now

The stencils I bought were the bendable cardboard kind, which are good for when the curb you're painting is curved. However I wanted the **inter-locking brass stencils** for flat curbs. I also wanted these because they inter-lock and stay in place, rather than having to tape each number together (see how they snap together?):

51

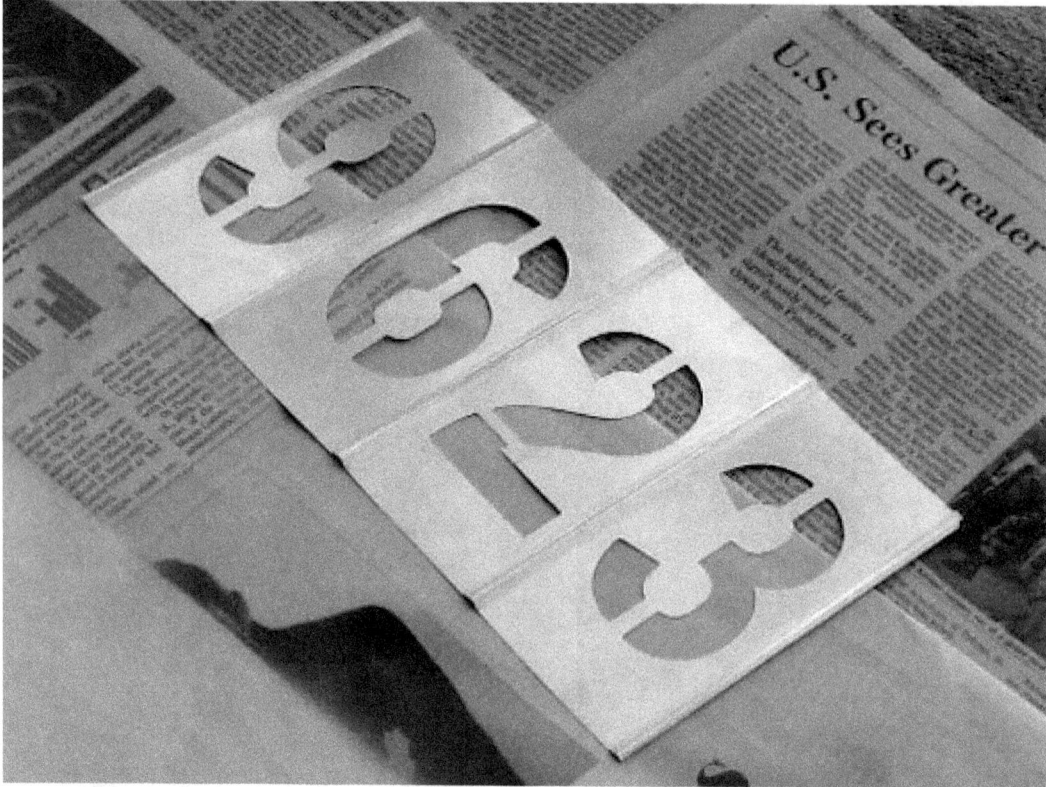

Next I tried a practice run on some more newspaper using the new materials I bought and the new brass stencils. It came out pretty descent:

I wanted to try another live run, so I looked no further than across the street at an old house.

If the police, fire department or ambulance service was looking for this house at night, it'd be VERY hard to see this address label. So next, I wanted to prove how much better a raggedy old curb address looks when painted over. I purposely used a smaller border to show this was the same curb, just painted over it for dramatic effect.

Look at the results of my test-run:

54

Look at the difference! You can still see the original outline I left as a comparison. THIS is why people will buy this service.

Here's some ideas for other small hustles you can do while going around door-to-door (if you have the balls).....

- Install peep holes on doors that don't have them. All it takes is some peep holes ($2/piece) and a drill with the correct size for your peep holes (steal a cordless drill from your dad's tool chest)!
- Weed a gardens
- Powerwash homes.

If you're already doing something for someone's home (like painting their curb number)...it's VERY easy to up-sell them into buying some other needed service like the list above.

Chapter 6
The Facebook Site

How I made a Facebook fan site, got a lot of traffic to it, almost got sued by
Facebook (and got a friend fired from Facebook), then sold the site.

Back in college I made a bunch of different advertising-only websites.

The idea was you make a website that people would come to, put some Google
Adsense ads on the side, and collect the money from when people click on the
ads.

Generally if you provided a nifty tool or interesting blog you could get reasonable
traffic for free (from search engines and others spreading the word about the
site).

The most fun one I did was a site called **FacebookProfile.com**, which was a
Facebook tips/tricks/fan site (it doesn't exist anymore).

At the time, Facebook was a social networking site with **massive** popularity
amongst the college population (and no one outside it).

Facebook was pretty popular, but not NEARLY as popular as it is today. It was
in the "gaining steam" phase at the time.

I had previously Google'd some Facebook tips and tricks….and really found
NEXT TO NOTHING about it. There were few posts in random forums about
some easy Facebook hacks and tricks…but not a single destination where
everything-Facebook was discussed.

This is where the idea for FacebookProfile.com spawned from.

I used the Google Keyword Tool to see what the most searched phrase for
Facebook was…..and "Facebook Profile" was the top. It turns out the domain
name FacebookProfile.com was available…..so I snagged it and started getting
the site built!

I wanted the site to be on the Wordpress platform, and I wanted it to **look and
feel like Facebook.**

I didn't have the skillzz necessary to create a custom Wordpress layout….so I
Photoshopped a mockup of exactly how the site should look and sent it to a
programmer.

FACEBOOK SCREENSHOT:

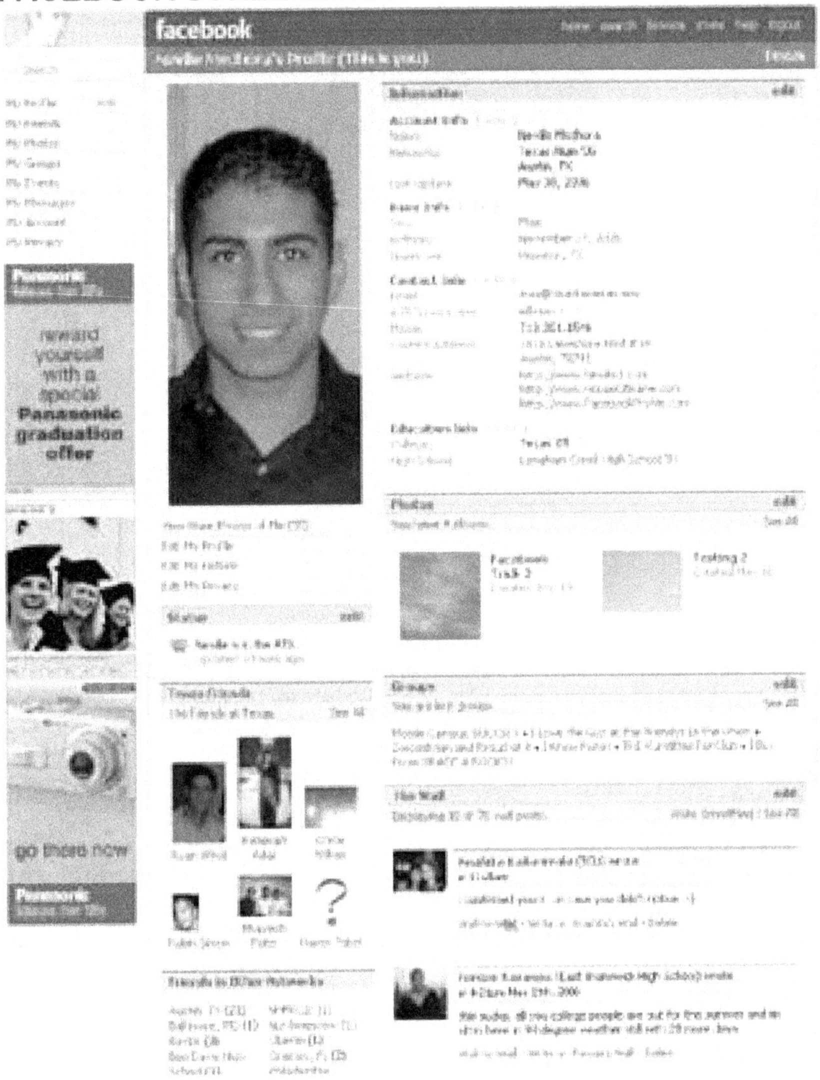

FACEBOOKPROFILE.COM
SCREENSHOT:

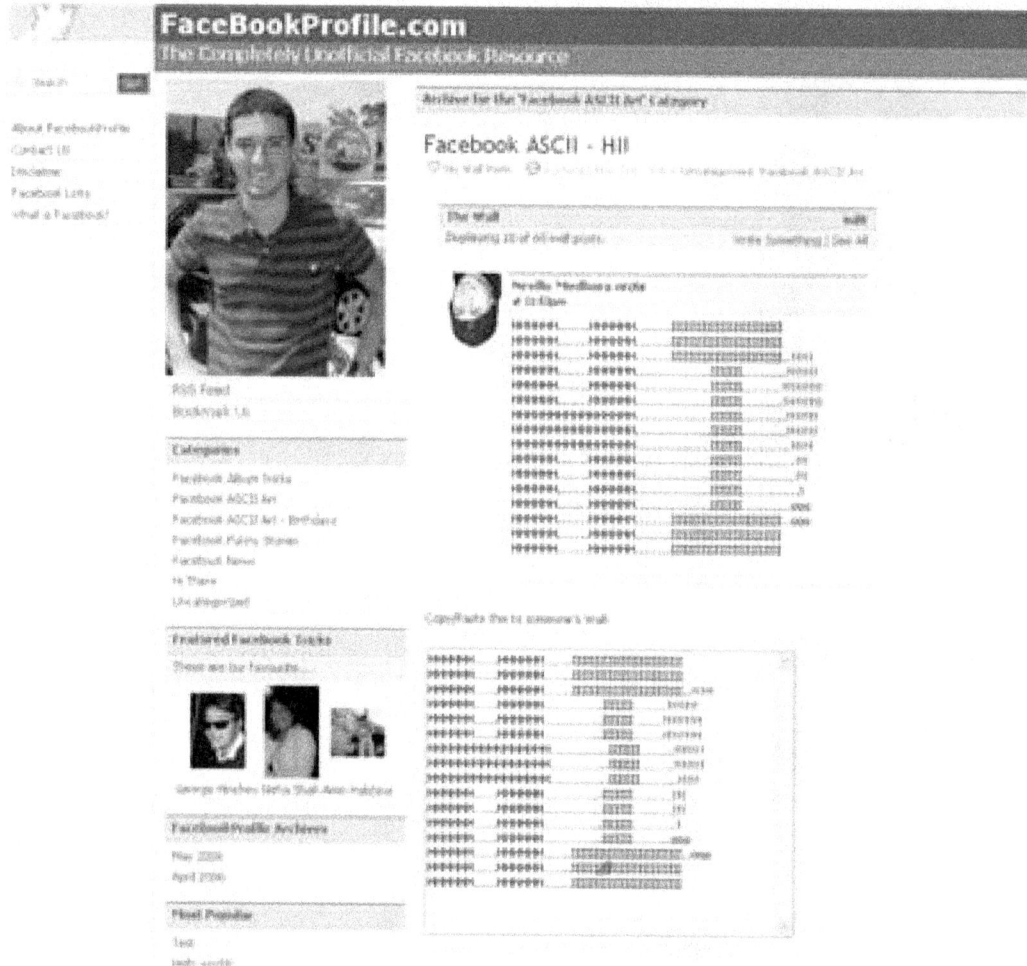

Since I already Photoshopped the site and knew EXACTLY what it should look like, the programmer cost me only $220 to make the full site.

The site turned out great....it pretty much looked exactly like Facebook did at the time!

I did this so people would know IMMEDIATEY they were on a Facebook-related website.

I posted a couple of articles on the site....such as some Facebook Hacks, Facebook Tricks.....and the main thing:

Facebook ASCII art.

You see, at the time you couldn't post pictures onto people Facebook "Wall".
Only text.

I used to write "Happy Birthday" on everyone's Facebook wall…but it was so
BORING because everyone wrote the same thing!

So I made this custom ASCII Art (it's just art made out of text characters) that
looked like this:

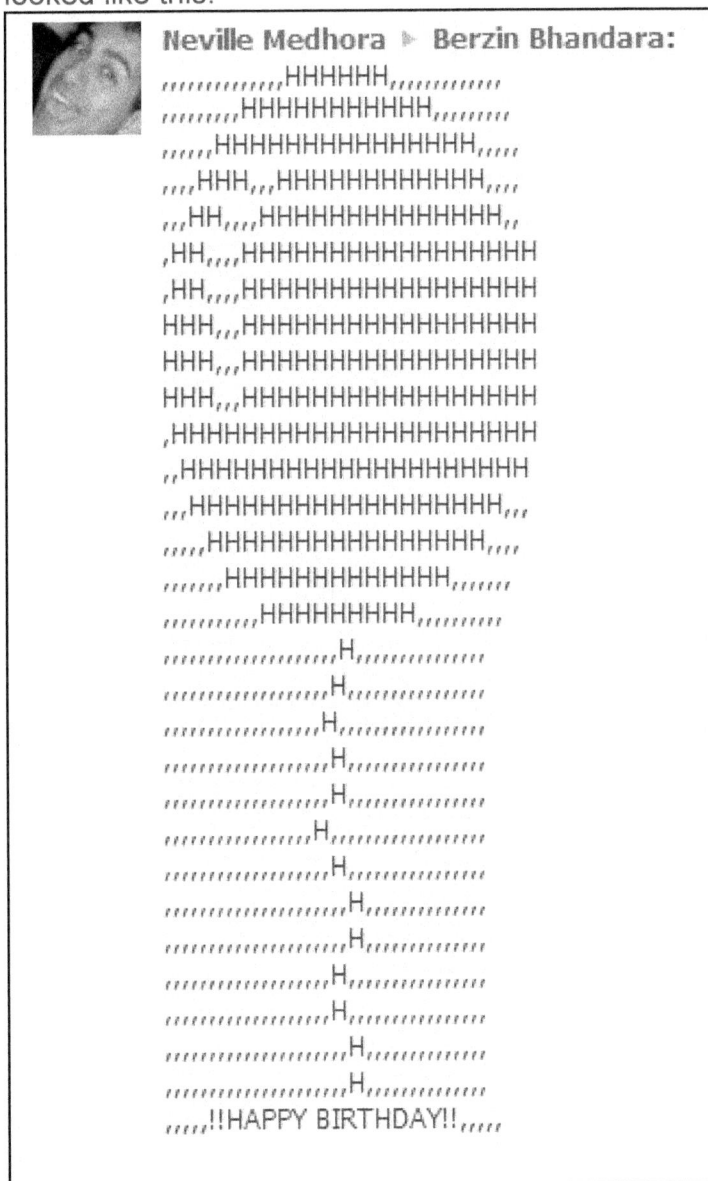

```
Neville Medhora ▶ Berzin Bhandara:
,,,,,,,,,,,,,HHHHHH,,,,,,,,,,,,
,,,,,,,,,,HHHHHHHHHH,,,,,,,,,
,,,,,,HHHHHHHHHHHHHH,,,,,
,,,,HHH,,,HHHHHHHHHHHH,,,,
,,,HH,,,,HHHHHHHHHHHHHH,,
,HH,,,,HHHHHHHHHHHHHHHHH
,HH,,,,HHHHHHHHHHHHHHHHHH
HHH,,,HHHHHHHHHHHHHHHHHH
HHH,,,HHHHHHHHHHHHHHHHHH
HHH,,,HHHHHHHHHHHHHHHHHH
,HHHHHHHHHHHHHHHHHHHHHH
,,HHHHHHHHHHHHHHHHHHHH
,,,HHHHHHHHHHHHHHHHHHH,,,
,,,,,HHHHHHHHHHHHHHHHH,,,,
,,,,,,,HHHHHHHHHHHHH,,,,,,,
,,,,,,,,,,HHHHHHHHH,,,,,,,,,,
,,,,,,,,,,,,,,,,,,,H,,,,,,,,,,,,,,,
,,,,,,,,,,,,,,,,,,H,,,,,,,,,,,,,,,,
,,,,,,,,,,,,,,,,,H,,,,,,,,,,,,,,,,,
,,,,,,,,,,,,,,,,,H,,,,,,,,,,,,,,,,,
,,,,,,,,,,,,,,,,,H,,,,,,,,,,,,,,,,,
,,,,,,,,,,,,,,,,H,,,,,,,,,,,,,,,,,,
,,,,,,,,,,,,,,,,H,,,,,,,,,,,,,,,,,
,,,,,,,,,,,,,,,,,H,,,,,,,,,,,,,,,
,,,,,,,,,,,,,,,,,H,,,,,,,,,,,,,
,,,,,,,,,,,,,,,,,H,,,,,,,,,,,,,,
,,,,,,,,,,,,,,,,,H,,,,,,,,,,,,,,,
,,,,,,,,,,,,,,,,,H,,,,,,,,,,,,,,
,,,,,,,,,,,,,,,,,H,,,,,,,,,,,,,
,,,,,!!HAPPY BIRTHDAY!!,,,,,
```

It was WAY more impactful than just saying:

"Happy Birthday!"

I posted that ASCII balloon and a whole bevvy of ASCII arts on the site....all of them made by me.

VERY QUICKLY THE SITE STARTED GETTING A LOT OF TRAFFIC!

Pretty much any inquiry on Google that said "Facebook ASCII" or "Facebook Hacks" would come straight to my site.

In the first few days of its existence it started getting about 200+ unique visitors per day!

Day	Hits		Files		Pages		Visits		Sites		KBytes	
1	7219	14.41%	4143	13.12%	1480	14.11%	234	12.86%	209	17.15%	116115	12.48%
2	6226	12.42%	4282	13.56%	1099	10.48%	251	13.80%	249	20.43%	125575	13.49%
3	4482	8.94%	2687	8.51%	898	8.56%	179	9.84%	150	12.31%	76167	8.18%
4	4009	8.00%	3029	9.59%	782	7.46%	166	9.13%	157	12.88%	88692	9.53%
5	4449	8.88%	3303	10.46%	891	8.50%	194	10.67%	209	17.15%	95522	10.26%
6	5699	11.37%	3200	10.13%	1217	11.60%	212	11.65%	180	14.77%	91171	9.80%
7	6342	12.66%	3913	12.39%	1366	13.02%	204	11.21%	172	14.11%	118096	12.69%
8	10656	21.26%	6365	20.15%	2471	23.56%	346	19.02%	193	15.83%	197155	21.18%

Daily Statistics for June 2006

Then in a few weeks the site started getting 400+ .....then 700+ unique visitors per day!

It was neat to get traffic so quickly, without putting too much effort into it.

I even would play little advertising stunts and write FACEBOOKPROFILE.COM all over the chalkboards in my college classes:

It was hilarious watching students pile in the room before class….and see EVERYONE open their laptops and type in "FacebookProfile.com" out of curiosity :-)

Soon the traffic was at 2,800+ unique visits per day!

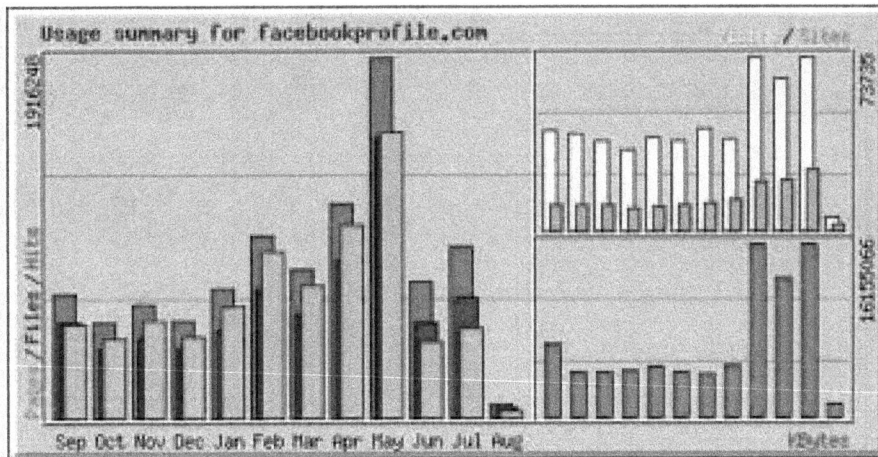

Usage summary for facebookprofile.com

Summary by Month

Month	Daily Avg					Monthly Totals				
	Hits	Files	Pages	Visits	Sites	KBytes	Visits	Pages	Files	Hits
Aug 2007	23917	16829	12570	1834	2586	1227685	5504	37711	50489	71753
Jul 2007	29466	20621	15492	2378	25750	16155066	73735	480265	639272	913446
Jun 2007	24219	16793	13347	2138	21222	12858705	64165	400436	503810	726571
May 2007	61814	47827	4899	2374	20718	16073210	73620	1518893	1482644	1916248
Apr 2007	37838	27867	3401	1297	13058	4896478	38934	1020451	836035	1135151
Mar 2007	25382	17773	22793	1384	11890	3974409	42933	706628	550973	786853
Feb 2007	34507	24488	31486	1368	10878	4187301	38327	881613	685685	966215
Jan 2007	21988	15111	19016	1285	10131	4639551	39838	589517	468460	681636
Dec 2006	16639	11923	13857	1111	9231	4372343	34442	429571	369625	515828
Nov 2006	19930	13989	17228	1276	11129	4125829	38300	516859	419676	597915
Oct 2006	16435	11619	13633	1313	11040	4270465	40712	422751	360195	509511
Sep 2006	21749	16954	16434	1413	11112	6798950	42411	493025	508631	652498
Totals						83579995	532921	7497720	6875495	9473625

63

Day	Hits		Files		Pages		Visits		Sites		KBytes	
1	21929	2.40%	15328	2.40%	11798	2.46%	1960	2.66%	984	3.82%	388137	2.40%
2	27076	2.96%	19095	2.99%	15147	3.15%	2237	3.03%	1090	4.23%	463657	2.87%
3	25912	2.84%	17781	2.78%	13939	2.90%	2213	3.00%	1064	4.13%	449050	2.78%
4	18303	2.00%	12482	1.95%	10430	2.17%	1719	2.33%	844	3.28%	318705	1.97%
5	15027	1.65%	10597	1.66%	8438	1.76%	1489	2.02%	763	2.96%	277324	1.72%
6	17834	1.95%	12735	1.99%	9577	1.99%	1733	2.35%	937	3.64%	319980	1.98%
7	23222	2.54%	15962	2.50%	11995	2.50%	2083	2.82%	1074	4.17%	436838	2.70%
8	34488	3.78%	24195	3.78%	17641	3.67%	3067	4.16%	1376	5.34%	654964	4.05%
9	40043	4.38%	28175	4.41%	21047	4.38%	3210	4.35%	1531	5.95%	740614	4.58%
10	38229	4.19%	27260	4.26%	20479	4.26%	3159	4.28%	1455	5.65%	678291	4.20%
11	36435	3.99%	25779	4.03%	19401	4.04%	2854	3.87%	1367	5.31%	650867	4.03%
12	33414	3.66%	23377	3.66%	17356	3.61%	2564	3.48%	1332	5.17%	609895	3.78%
13	32383	3.55%	22726	3.55%	17520	3.65%	2613	3.54%	1301	5.05%	569381	3.52%
14	24457	2.68%	16941	2.65%	12961	2.70%	2083	2.82%	1069	4.15%	434116	2.69%
15	25830	2.83%	18567	2.90%	13713	2.86%	2182	2.96%	1108	4.30%	438863	2.72%
16	34371	3.76%	24292	3.80%	17830	3.71%	2614	3.55%	1376	5.34%	581456	3.60%
17	35397	3.88%	24519	3.84%	17766	3.70%	2835	3.84%	1481	5.75%	607696	3.76%
18	34860	3.82%	23361	3.65%	18368	3.82%	2705	3.67%	1350	5.24%	621997	3.85%
19	21567	2.36%	15368	2.40%	11218	2.34%	1811	2.46%	937	3.64%	377156	2.33%
20	28173	3.08%	20120	3.15%	14825	3.09%	2242	3.04%	1176	4.57%	485708	3.01%
21	25367	2.78%	17634	2.76%	13324	2.77%	2080	2.82%	951	3.69%	455496	2.82%
22	27764	3.04%	19345	3.03%	14644	3.05%	2221	3.01%	1023	3.97%	495871	3.07%
23	38671	4.23%	26792	4.19%	19820	4.13%	2924	3.97%	1346	5.23%	671155	4.15%
24	38690	4.24%	26879	4.20%	19671	4.10%	2847	3.86%	1357	5.27%	681188	4.22%
25	38560	4.22%	26749	4.18%	19788	4.12%	2835	3.84%	1397	5.43%	668790	4.14%
26	36020	3.94%			18964	3.95%	2849	3.86%	1385	5.38%	637933	3.95%
27	11400	1.25%	8049	1.26%			952	1.29%	499	1.94%	208620	1.29%
28			17554		13190	2.75%	1942	2.63%	1002	3.89%	457104	2.83%
29	29826	3.27%	21142	3.31%	15556	3.24%	2358	3.20%	1279	4.97%	520681	3.22%
30	36477	3.99%	25518	3.99%	19039	3.96%	2872	3.90%	1390	5.40%	632041	3.91%
31	36365	3.98%	26162	4.09%	18713	3.90%	2728	3.70%	1417	5.50%	621491	3.85%

Now I had a site that organically made it's way to about 3,000 unique visits per day……but unfortunately I WAS AN IDIOT at this time in my life.

I had not yet studied marketing and how to make money from a high-traffic website.

The only way I made money from FacebookProfile.com was the little side-bar with Google Adsense on the side.

It would sit there and make $100+ per month....and I thought that was just fine and dandy.

I didn't build an email list.

I didn't sell advertising spots.

I didn't have a weekly newsletter.

I didn't ask people to share the site with their friends.

Overall I just did a horrible job at marketing (because I didn't know SQUAT about it at the time).

Had I known what I know now.....the site might still exist and would generate a pretty significant income.

Since this website experiment was openly talked about on my blog….almost immediately after I discussed the traffic I was getting and money I was making….**PEOPLE STARTED TO COPY IT.**

I openly posted the full mockup of the site, detailed development document and how I got it outsources….so people literally copied the website!

What really infuriated me though was people simply ripped all the content off my site.

It bugged me to no end….but ultimately there was little I could do.

I still FAR outranked any of the copy-cats, but it was still a nagging thing to deal with.

Anywhoozle, I eventually decided to sell the site because I'd lost interest and wasn't really updating it.

Facebook Apps had just come out, and tens of thousands of new people were joining Facebook EVERYDAY....so I figured this would be the perfect time to sell it.

I simple posted it on SitePoint (a large community of webmasters that had a great place to sell websites) and immediately got a good amount of interest.

Ultimately the site sold for $5,500 (which is a cool sum of money for a college student).

Buying Domain	-$10
Designer	-$220
Hosting	$0
Transfer Fees	$0
TOTAL COST	-$230
FacebookProfile Sale	5,500
TOTAL PROFIT from sale	$5,270

However this profit doesn't include the Adsense revenue the site brought in. So every month I owned the site, it sent a few hundred dollars my way.

So this little "experiment" churned out several hundred dollars a month for a year, and eventually sold for $5,500. Plus I learned a lot about Wordpress, SEO and traffic generation from it!

So a funny side-note from this site was:

VERY SOON after I created this FacebookProfile.com site, the fine people at Facebook actually sent an email message to everyone in the company about it (including Mark Zuckerberg)!

At the time Facebook was about 40 people in size.

They apparently liked the site….but eventually sent me a package with a cease-and-desist from using the domain FacebookProfile.com and using trademarked terms such as "Wall" on my site (I re-named "comments" on the site to "Wall posts").

Facebook also claimed my site "HIGHLY RESEMBLED" Facebook.com (which it totally did).

In fact, a lot of people thought my site WAS Facebook since the design was the exact same! Ha!

Anywho….my friend Noah worked at Facebook at the time (he was employee number 30-something)….so I called him up and told him this site was a Facebook FAN site and not meant to steal traffic from Facebook. It was made to make Facebook more enjoyable!

He "handled" things on his end….and it seemed the problem was solved.

Two days later…**NOAH GOT FIRED!**

I still don't know if it was because of what he did for me, or something else (I'm guessing a little of Column A and a little of Column B).

Chapter 6
My Affiliate Marketing Experiment

How I kept reading about stupid "affiliate marketing" crap and decided to try it to see why everyone in the industry was so shady.

I spend a STUPIDLY large amount of time online reading, working, horsing around etc....and I run across the term **"Affiliate Marketing"** all the time. I even go to an "internet marketing" event once a month here in Austin to meet other entrepreneurs, but always found some of the people doing affiliate marketing a little perplexing (aka REALLY SHADY).

When prying into what they do, they never gave me CLEAR answers. They would always say things like, "I do lead generation" or "performance marketing" or "sell an online product" and other buzzwords I didn't fully understand.

I'd ask, **"Ok, give me an example of a product you generate leads for"** and they'd state a general industry at most (such as insurance, health or real estate). Some of the people said they do "PPC arbitrage" and that they "promote products" but wouldn't go much further into detail about their business.

I was never satisfied with these responses and just presumed these people were really shady (which some of them are).

So here I am trying to find out what these people do and they keep skirting around the actual details...WHAT THE HELL?

I can tell them I own a rave store called HouseOfRave.com and sell light up stuff online. Its pretty straightforward, and they can even see the website for themselves. Why were these people acting so shady? They were obviously hiding something or lying about something.

Many of the people I met in the affiliate marketing world seemed to sell herbal pills online or get rich quick schemes for the masses. Most of the products they were promoting seemed **relatively useless** once purchased, and most had "interesting" billing plans (you buy them for cheap, but somewhere in fine print you get billed every month for it).

In my mind, I saw "affiliate marketing" as referring to a website that promises to get you rich quick...something like this kind of crap:

The claims seems fake, misleading, and pander to the most desperate of people.

I've read many bloggers like John Chow and other guys who make their living from blogging and they frequently talk about affiliate marketing. **I kept wondering what exactly it was, especially since they get so much of their income to it**.....so I decided to do some research and find out.....

The first thing I did was research the term "Affiliate Marketing" and physically printed out all the articles I could find. I read them all and took notes on a plane ride somewhere.

I read the Wikipedia article and a bunch of other search results, and the most basic idea behind Affiliate Marketing is:

1. Someone is selling a product.
2. You help promote that product.
3. When someone buys a product through your recommendation, you get paid a percentage of the sale.

SIMPLE.

I thought about this for a second and realized there are many successful companies that heavily use affiliate marketing in a non-shady way. These include Amazon, eBay and so many others. Amway and other companies also use an affiliate structure. Even car dealerships to a small extent seemed like "affiliates" of their larger companies like Toyota and Ford.

The easiest example I can give of a super-simple affiliate marketing experiment is the Book Review Page on my blog. If you click one of those book links and buy from Amazon, **I get a small portion of the sale.** Amazon is willing to do this because I helped drive a sale to their site through my review. **If it weren't for me, they probably wouldn't have made that sale.**

So THAT was affiliate marketing?? Not completely.

A lot of people I met talked about buying ads to promote their affiliate products....this was part of the term "Pay-Per-Click Arbitrage" I heard so much about. Some of the more intelligent people in the internet marketing group I attend made a lot of their money this way. I found out what some of these people do is:

- Signup for an affiliate program for a product.
- Buy ads on Google, Yahoo, banner ads etc promoting these products.
- Clicks get sent directly to the product page or their own webpage promoting the product.
- Whenever a sale is made from that action, they get a percentage of the sale.

This is a frequently touted method of getting rich quick by many crappy eBooks. In essence it makes sense. **For Example:**

- If you buy paid clicks from Google costing $0.10/click.....
- You send all that traffic to a webpage that offers an affiliate product/service/signup...whatever.
- That service pays you $2 per transaction that succeeds.
- If 1 out of every ten people completes that offer, that costs you $1.00 at Google.
- So for every dollar you spend, you make two dollars.
- So long as your spending is less than your earnings, you're making money.

The math behind this actually works, and some people legitimately make a lot of money doing this....and that's why people buying get-rich-quick schemes believe in these methods.

I thought this affiliate marketing world was a good model at its essence, so why was everyone I met in this world always so shady? If these people were making money doing arbitrage, why didn't they share details?

Well.....I was being a tenacious little monkey and wanted to find out!

My favorite method of learning something is **jumping into it.** I'll usually start by reading all I can about a subject, then quickly try a real life version of something simple, then something more advanced....an "**experiment**" so to say.

So I wanted to try an **affiliate marketing experiment** in order to learn all about this industry. From what I understood, a lot of affiliate marketing had to do with creating effective landing pages and making people want to buy or take action.

Basically that means out of 100 visitors to a web page, how many of them can you make buy something or signup? Since I run an e-commerce store, this appealed to me. Perhaps learning some of this affiliate marketing could help me increase the effectiveness of my own business!

I decided to embark on this affiliate marketing experiment in my spare time for one month to see what I could learn. I first made a written list of things I wanted to learn from it:

- Learn why most affiliate marketers don't go into much detail about their work.
- Learn more about what all this affiliate marketing stuff is all about.
- Learn to make great and effective landing pages.
- Learn how to A/B split test landing pages using Google Website Optimizer.
- Further understand how to optimize paid keywords and conversion rates.

Even if my real life experiment lost money, this list contains some **pretty valuable skills that could add much benefit to my own business.** So I continued on….

Now to start a real life experiment promoting something!

So for the first part of this experiment I decided to try something *really simple* that could just be a proof of concept….just to see if it could work. I wanted to do a simple campaign where I promote an affiliate link over Google Adwords. When someone clicks through to the ad and buys, I get a commission. So long as I spend less to buy the ads than my commissions ad up to, I make money.

It works in theory, now to see if it works in action….

I could've either joined something like CJ.com or ClickBank.com to find affiliate offers to promote or find one myself. I decided to steer clear of the affiliate networks for this simple experiment solely to **find something easy to promote without tons of competition doing the same thing.**

I had seen some videos about a new thing called "electronic cigarettes" becoming popular in bars, and started Googling. I'm not a smoker, but this e-cig concept seemed like a brand new industry which has the potential to become big, but hasn't yet.

I did a little research on e-cigarettes and first joined the BluCigs.com affiliate program simply because they had the best looking marketing material and easiest-to-buy-from website (See that link for BluCigs.com in the previous sentence? On a website, that link would have my affiliate ID on it. THAT'S an affiliate link in action! If you buy after clicking that link, I make a commission).

So now they gave me an affiliate link to place on my advertisements like this: http://affiliate.blucigs.com/idevaffiliate.php?id=3257_0_3_1

Whenever you click that link, it takes you directly to the BluCigs website and if you make a purchase after you click that link, I make a commission!

Simple affiliate marketing in action. Understand?

I now have something to promote....e-cigarettes...and I don't even know a damn thing about them....but it doesn't matter.

Now a great way to get traffic is to make my own ecigarettes site and build up a readership over time, but this is supposed to be a **_quick_** experiment, so the best way to get traffic quick is to BUY IT.

Since e-cigarettes weren't such a massively popular keyword at the time, the traffic was dirt cheap. I could pay $0.05 per click and still be in the top results (or only result) for many keywords (which is why I chose something with low competition).

I immediately made a couple of Google AdWords ads and posted them. Here was one of them:

Results 1 - 100 of about **1,230,000** for **blu cig** (0.42 seconds)

garette
like a real **cigarette**. Make the switch today to **blu**,
tronic **Cigarette** look and ...
rvice - Affiliates

E-**Cigarette** - How it Works
d inhale, the blue LED light at the tip glows like a real
king. ...
p - Cached - Similar

blucigs.com

- e-**cigarette**-forum.com • The place ...
yesterday. My initial reaction to it: whoa! the pack for it
rger for it. its all very.
garettes/22993-blu-cig-review-comparison.html -

5, 2009
8, 2009
_____ - Aug 8, 2009
im.com »

Sponsored Links

Go Blu
Only visit when you're ready to buy
Free shipping through this link!
www.BluCigsStore.com

The "Sponsored Link" on the right points to my link.

Once again…Whenever you click that sponsored link, it takes you directly to the BluCigs website and if you make a purchase after you click that link, I make a commission!

Simple affiliate marketing in action again!
Understand yet?

So now I just sit back and waste money on buying traffic to see if I make a sale. I thought this would take longer than it did, but sure enough in about 2 days I **made my first sale!** The BluCigs program gives me 20% of each sale, and it was a $59.95 sale, netting me $11.99 in commission….so far I'd only spent about $0.50 in ads! Pretty good return on investment!

This 24X return on investment was on an extremely small scale, so I was excited to see if that pace would keep up. However if it does, you see how certain people can make lots of commissions with very little spending?

A day or two later, I made ANOTHER SALE for $104.95, netting me a total of $20.99 in commissions! Even though this isn't a whole lot of money, I was excited my dinky little experiment was giving a good ROI (return on investment).

Using less than $5 I now made $32.98 back!

At this point I still didn't even really know what an e-cigarette was, but I was making money off them.

Cool......but the party was soon halted.

Google AdWords slapped my hand in the beginning of this experiment saying my ad was declined because it contained cigarette-related terms which are not allowed to be advertised. I changed the text so it never says "cigarette" or any closely-related term:

If you're buying BluCigs
and want free shipping,
Use this link to buy!
www.BluCigs.com

This worked for two days, then Google denied the ad again saying the link-to URL was different than what was advertised (I guess since I had the referral link in it) so they asked me to change it.

Unfortunately I couldn't get Google to accept my ad anymore.....I've been doing an affiliate marketing experiment for only a few days and ALREADY I was caught for doing something shady!! HA!

Well, Google has a fair policy to ensure quality, so I decided an alternate and perfectly OK way of doing this was....

I bought a domain called BluCigsStore.com (if you recall the actually website is called BluCigs.com, without the suffix "Store") and made an auto-direct script for the page to forward to my affiliate link.

I immediately changed the banned ad to BluCigsStore.com and Google accepted the changes, I was back in business!

This cost me about $19 to privately register the domain name (so my name is not immediately associated with it).

A problem I noticed earlier was if people browsed around the internet researching these BluCigs, they would invariably click on several affiliate links.

Whoever was the LAST affiliate link gets the commission. Blast.

To help improve my odds of being that person, I made a simple frames page (just used a template in Microsoft FrontPage since I can't even write simple HTML). Nothing shady or illegal about this, and it actually added some value to the customer because it makes it easier for them to navigate. I used Photoshop to make the graphic for the frame header, and FrontPage to create the simple frames page and picture-link the graphic.

Now when you go to BluCigsStore.com you see the normal store with a static header on it that doesn't move. When you click around the site, that header stays up. If you want to navigate home, it has a button for that. It also has an EXIT button that is a link to my affiliate link:

Just that little strip of webpage at the top is mine. The rest is just BluCigs.com

Using that frame bar on my own browser made it easier for me to navigate the BluCigs.com site, so I'm guessing other people probably found it helpful (and probably never expected it was an affiliate tactic)!

So Google once again approved my ads and I started making more money….

…so now I had a very simple yet profitable affiliate campaign running. The next step was to try out some of the other e-cigarette companies with affiliate programs. I found another good e-cig company called GreenSmoke and joined their affiliate program.

I already knew what to do (and not to do) thanks to my prior BluCigs experiment, so I quickly setup my GreenSmoke campaign:

- I registered a domain called BuyGreenSmokes.com
- PhotoShopped a custom frames header for it that made it seem like part of the GreenSmoke website.
- I made the framed header like my BluCigsStore site and got the new site running.
- Immediately got some Google AdWords pointing towards it.

Since I already knew what to do, within about **1 hour I completed most of this work.** When BuyGreenSmokes.com went live it looked like:

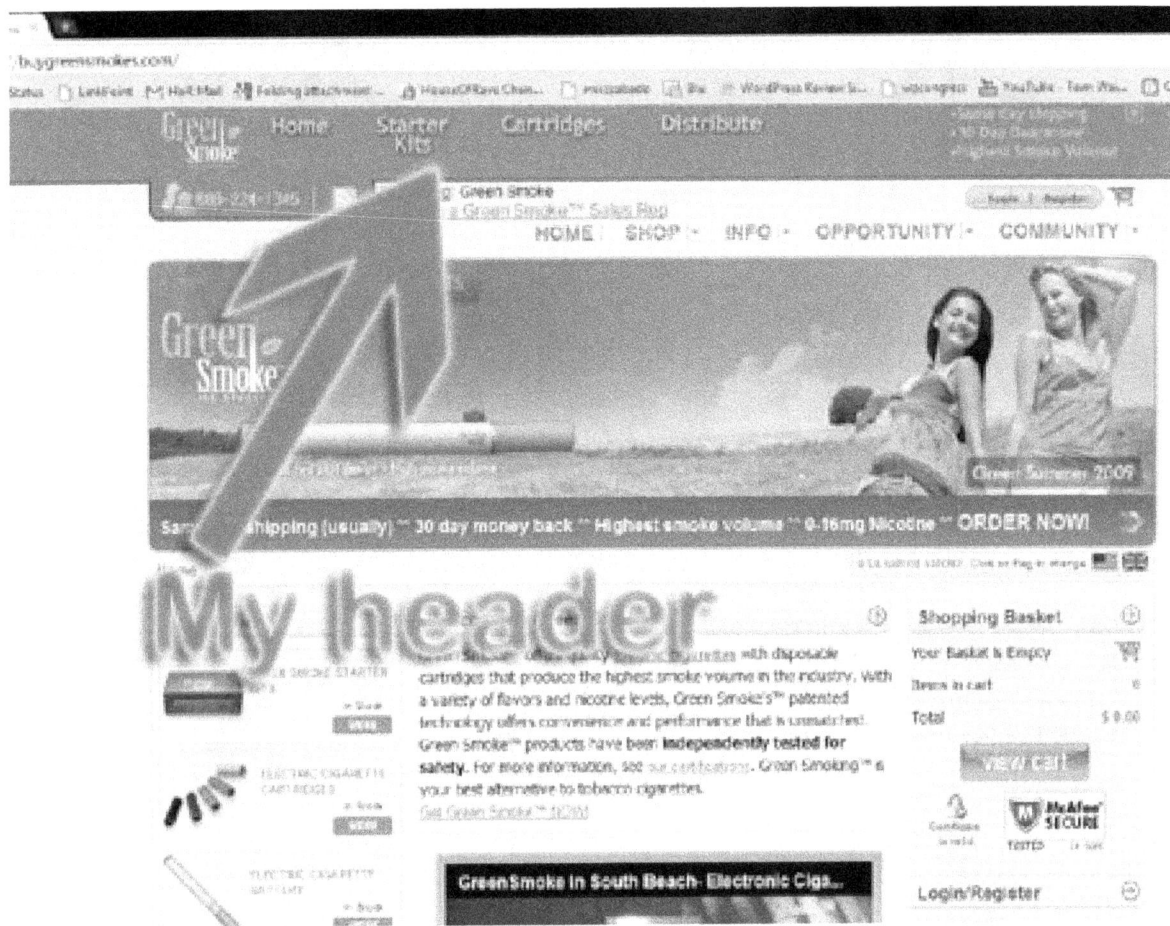

So just like the BluCigs page I made, anytime someone gets to this page through my link and buys something, **I make money!**

Speaking of the BluCigs experiment, whilst I was making the GreenSmoke page and signing up for other affiliate programs….this small little experiment of mine had been making 1-2 sales per day from the BluCigs campaign, and within a few days here was my revenue:

blu affiliate center.

Welcome Neville Medhora
Your Affiliate ID: 3257
Log out of Affiliate Central

Stats

	Pending	Cleared	Total
Transactions	15	4	19
Sales	$954.05	$189.80	$1,143.85
Commission	$190.81	$37.96	$228.77

- Cleared transactions are based on orders that have been shipped
- Pending transactions are based on open orders that have not been shipped
- Orders that have been canceled, refunded (credited) or voided are not included

Clickthroughs	
Clicks	324
Conversion Rate	5.86%

At this time for every dollar I spent on AdWords, I was making $6 back. So a **6X Return on Investment.** At this point I had never seen the product I sold or promoted, didn't know anything about them and wasn't particularly "helping" anyone.

In fact, the people who came through my links never knew who I was or that they were coming through an affiliate!

However in about a week I earned my first check:

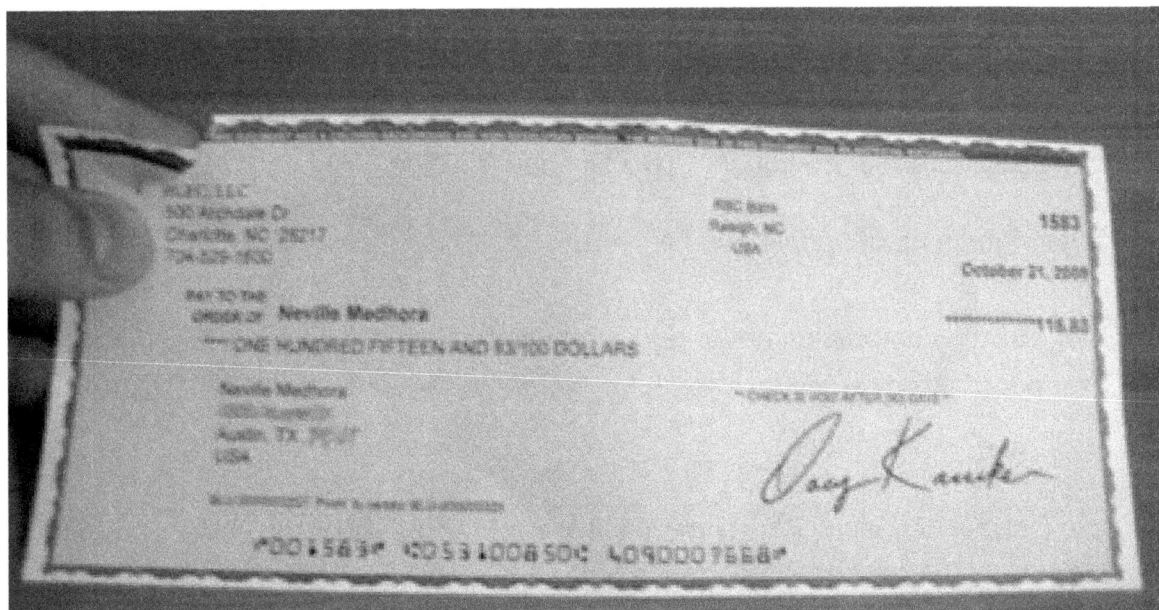

This is a very simple affiliate experiment, and probably against the rules of most affiliate offers. You see, I'm not ACTUALLY adding any value to the companies whose products I'm promoting. They probably would've made these sales if I was in the picture or not.

Now lets say I owned a large forum for smokers to talk about smoking....and I write an article about how great BluCigs or GreenSmoke electronic cigarettes are. If those articles contained affiliate links that people followed then purchased products, THAT would be of great value to the companies....they just made sales they probably wouldn't have without me.

NOW REWIND BACK to the first part of this experiment, I was talking about why a lot of affiliate marketers seemed **shady**:

> *"I can tell them I own an online rave store that sells light up stuff online. It's pretty straightforward, and they can even see the website for themselves. Why were these people acting so shady? They were obviously hiding something or lying about something."*

From this little experiment the answer became glaringly obvious why these affiliate marketers wouldn't tell me EXACTLY what they were promoting:

They don't want competition!

If I told someone "I'm doing this easy affiliate program for BluCigs and making 6X my money!" ….what do you think would happen REALLY soon??

That's right, tons of people copying you.

Cool…a little competition never hurt. But what's different now is since there are other people bidding for your same keywords on your ads, the PRICE GOES UP.

Now instead of making 6X my money, I'm down to 2X all of a sudden….and if more people start bidding the price up, I might even start **losing** money soon.

So all of a sudden I'm making tons of cash, then one week later that same campaign is LOSING money. No wonder people keep their damn mouths shut!

So the first two questions of my **original list of things to learn** were mainly answered.

Now I wanted to learn about **making a good landing page** using Google Website Optimizer. This could be something I could use on my other businesses to make more money. All the while I was learning all these new things, I was still collecting about $100+ per week in commissions from this small-time experiment….

SO TO REFLECT ON WHAT I'VE LEARED SO FAR:

Pro's of simple affiliate marketing:
- It's possible to start making money very quickly with relatively little work.
- It's possible to scale up successful campaigns to large levels.
- It's possible to "sell" a product without knowing anything about it.

It's not hard to see why so many get-rich-quick books teach this very method of making money…because it SEEMS like it could work for anyone. Some people might even have some nominal success trying something like this, but very quickly the con's start showing their head:

Con's of simple affiliate marketing:
- It's possible to LOSE those quickly-gained profits very quickly.
- Most successful campaigns you create will start to garner much attention from other affiliate marketers who quickly start copying you.
- You have to be hush about your work....you can't openly talk about what you're promoting or your methods. This is why many people I talked to about this were so secretive.

By and far the largest con I see with doing this simple type of affiliate marketing is there is no long term value being provided. With my business HouseOfRave, everything I do today pays off for months at a time, even years.

With these small affiliate promotions, there is very little value ultimately being imparted to the customer. Ultimately a beginner trying to simply "make money online" with these almost-scam-like promotions will probably end up disappointed.

But screw that, I was now up to $371 in profit with JUST BluCigs and I'd barely spent $70 to get there! See:

blu affiliate center.

Welcome Neville Medhora
Your Affiliate ID: 3257
‑Log out of Affiliate Central

Stats

	Pending	Cleared	Total
Transactions	23	7	30
Sales	$1,540.70	$314.65	$1,855.35
Commission	$308.14	$62.93	$371.07

» Cleared transactions are based on orders that have been shipped
» Pending transactions are based on open orders that have not been shipped
» Orders that have been canceled, refunded (credited) or voided are not included

Clickthroughs	
Clicks	684
Conversion Rate	4.39%

….and this experiment called for finding out how to make a landing and optimize it with Google Website Optimizer, so that was the next step.

Basically what I'm trying to do in this step is **have several versions of the same page and measure the effectiveness of each.** After X-amount of people cycle through each version, a clear winner is usually identified. This is called an A/B Split Test…and if you do this enough, you can identify which pages convert the most people.

For this I had to do several things:
- Make a separate landing page to send traffic (I chose ecigaretterecs.com).
- Make three different versions of the page.
- Enter all this stuff into Google Website Optimizer.
- Drive traffic to the site, wait for results.

I didn't say this experiment was going to be pretty, I just wanted to learn the underlying lessons in it, so here goes:

I chose ecigaretterecs.com because all other domain name combinations were taken. Ultimately it didn't matter what the domain was…this was just a ghetto experiment. I setup the site on my server and was up and running.

I wanted a basic page that looked sort of like a reviews site….a site where you go to get reviews of a particular genre of product. I actually first purchased a **WordPress plugin** that makes a fully-functional reviews site, but I wanted this experiment to be extremely quick and dirty so I did it the ghetto home-made way.

Since E-cigarettes are quite new, there are multiple brands people want to look through before choosing one. I would provide this review information for them on this (ghetto and poorly made) page (ecigaretterecs.com).

I decided I would make three very different versions: 1 stylish, 1 simple and plan, 1 supper-ghetto:

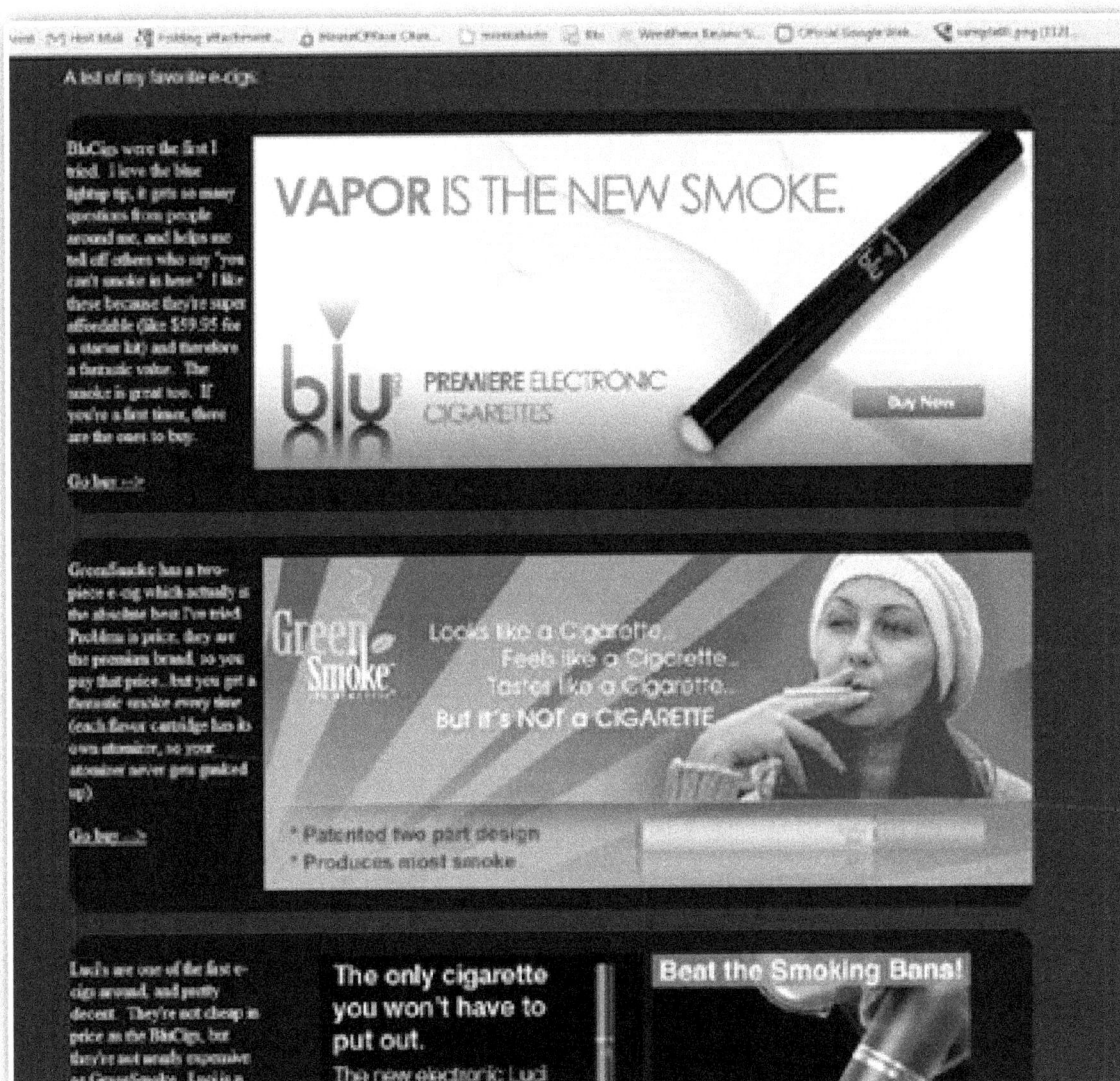

(This was the "stylish" one…shut up, don't make fun of my web design skilzz)!

Monkey/Desktop/blu/landing%20page/index2.html

Reviews and recommendations of the best e-cigarettes.

There's so many brands it gets hard to choose. We've put our favorites here for others to share. Less researching, more smoking.
~eCigaretteRecs.com

BluCigs were the first I tried. I love the blue lightup tip, it gets so many questions from people around me, and helps me tell off others who say "you can't smoke in here." I like these because they're super affordable (like $59.95 for a starter kit) and therefore a fantastic value. The smoke is great too. If you're a first timer, there are the ones to buy.

Click below to visit:

VAPOR IS THE NEW SMOKE.

blu **PREMIERE ELECTRONIC CIGARETTES**

Buy Now

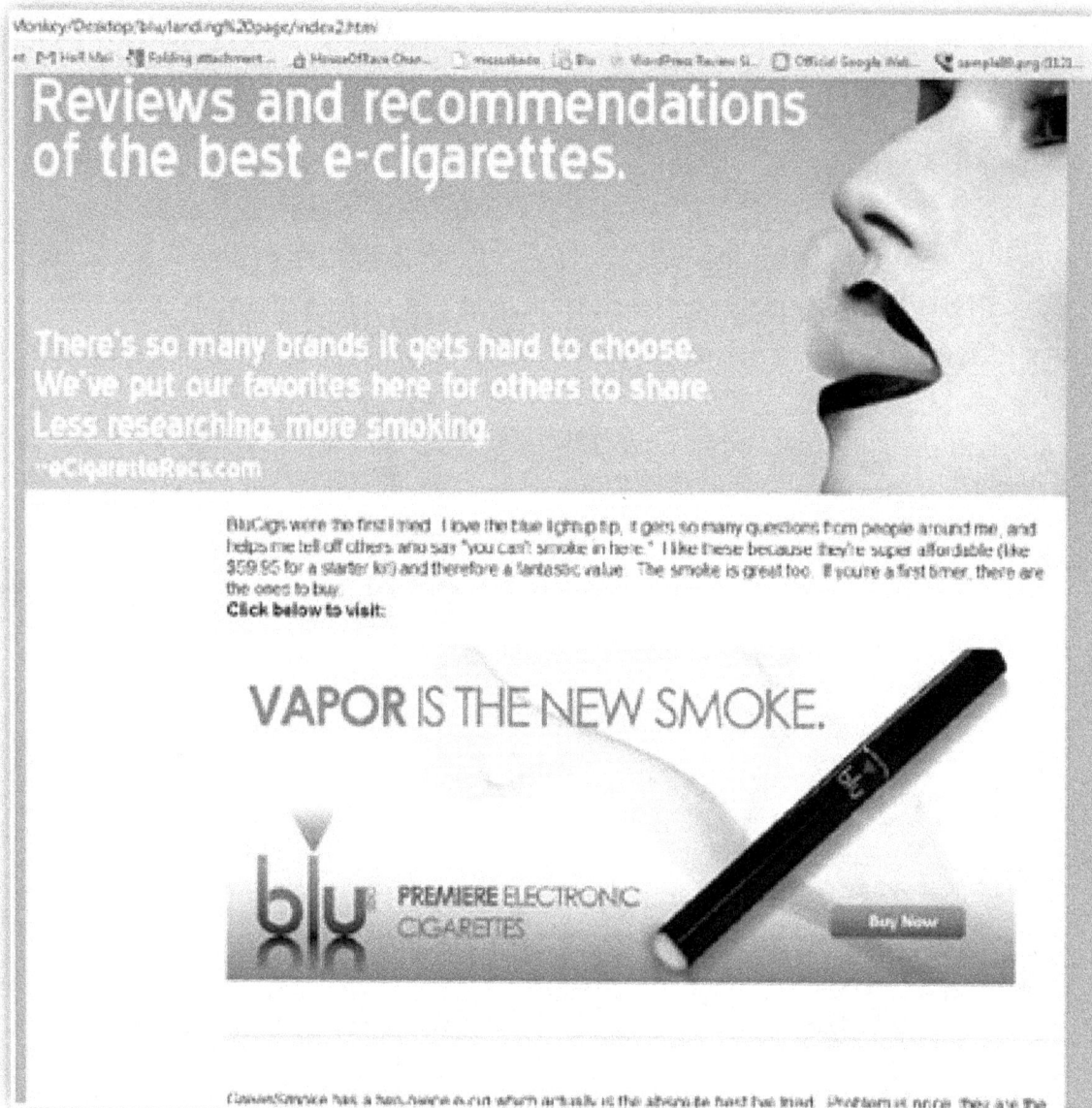

(This was "plain and simple").

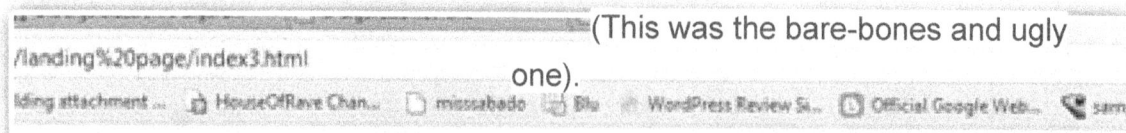

(This was the bare-bones and ugly one).

/landing%20page/index3.html

…the point of this is to simply **test out different versions and see if there was any statistical difference in how each of them converted into sales.**

Sometimes the data is very surprising. I find from many friends who do this on a large scale that **ugly and simply is often better.**

SIDE NOTE: ...were the first I tried. I love the blue lightup tip, it gets so many questions from people around me, and helps me tell off others who say "you can't smoke in here." I like these because they're super affordable (like $59.95 for a starter kit) and therefore a fantastic value. The smoke is great too. If you're a first timer, there are the

An A/B Split Test doesn't need to have versions that are so dramatically different like this experiment, The different versions can simply have different headline text or font type.

I went through the Google Optimizer process and outfitted each version of the page with special snippets of code (keep in mind this is something almost ANYONE can do) and set all the links to go to the affiliate sites I earlier created with the custom headers.

Now when someone lands on the webpage ecigaretterecs.com, it randomly selects which version of that page to show the visitor. So if you look at that page from your computer and your friend views it from a different computer, there is a good chance you will see a completely different page.

Google Website Optimizer then collects information over time and tracks the conversion rates to see if there is a statistically "better" version. When I ended up pulling the plug on this experiment there were only 190 page visits, but no statistical variance shown (you usually need around 50 conversions per variant before conclusions can be drawn).

I didn't get the final results before I pulled the plug on this experiment, **but I didn't care.** I had learned how to A/B Split Test which was the important thing….now I can use it to make already-profitable pages more profitable.

So far I've accomplished almost everything I set out to learn with this experiment, and I even made some money while at it!

I was still making money, so why did I finally end up pulling the plug on this experiment?

….so eventually I pulled the plug on this little experiment (it ran for roughly 5 weeks).

One of the negative parts about affiliate marketing I mentioned was the price of Pay-Per-Click varies wildly, especially when people are bidding up keywords. This can be the difference between a profit and loss if you don't watch out. This happened several times and the cost I had to pay shot up too much to be as profitable.

Basically I got these campaigns running for the experiment, but when I stopped paying attention, most of the good keywords stopped running because they exceeded my set budget. Eventually most traffic died down, a sale was made here and there, but nothing big.

Ultimately I ended up bringing in **$727** from the BluCigs campaign and **$360** from the GreenSmoke campaign (about 90% of that money was from that first 5 weeks) and paid a total of **$166** for Google Adsense.

A net profit of $921 (minus a little money for domain names). Not a bad profit for an EXPERIMENT that I figured would lose money!

I could have kept on going, but the amount of effort for a short-term profit wasn't worth it, especially when I already have profitable businesses of my own that offer a more long-term payoff. I can already see some of you trying to signup and start your own experiments with these ;-)

…however…hopefully this experiment demonstrated the POTENTIAL this sort of business model has in a more legitimate form. I wish I knew about it a long time ago when I was an active "financial" blogger.

I learned a lot and made a net profit!
-Neville Medhora

P.S. Something interesting to note is that BluCigs.com sent me affiliate checks every few weeks for about a year.

GreenSmoke.com TILL THIS DAY still send me checks ranging from $60 to $150 every month! It's from people I originally signed up, and when they buy again, I still get a commission!

The End!

This is where we both cry and say goodbye to each other.

Thanks for reading! I hope you not only enjoyed it, but also LEARNED.

While the goal of this book was to simply "see if I could write a book in two weeks" ....the REAL goal is to motivate people to do something.

I've seen soooo many people that've sought out my help with starting a business, and I used to offer advice, give book recommendations, and show people how my own business works.....but that pales in comparison to this advice:

If you want to learn to start a business.....just do something outside of a job that will make you $100 dollars.

That's it.

No seriously....THAT'S ALL THE ADVICE I HAVE.

I got that concept from my friend Mickey Ristroph.

In fact, his company was started by something like this (and now they have 180+ people in Austin, TX. alone)!

Him and some friends had been doing little "businesses" all through college. They thought of themselves as "business men" .....until it dawned on them that **none of their ideas or websites had ever produced any money!**

So they decided to just make ONE DOLLAR IN ONE MONTH.

That's it.
One measly little dollar....
....and a whole month to do it.

Needless to say they hit the goal....and then the goal was set to $100.

...and so forth. Now they are at tens of millions per year.

So if you haven't already.....go out there and make ONE LITTLE DOLLAR. The education you get from it will be priceless.
-Sincerely,
Neville N. Medhora
NevBlog.com

www.ingramcontent.com/pod-product-compliance
Lightning Source LLC
Chambersburg PA
CBHW051417200326
41520CB00023B/7270